FOR THE RECORD III

Still More ...

Encouraging Words for Ordinary Catholics

R. Puratt

─────── ℰᴆ ───────

Also by J. Ronald Knott

An Encouraging Word: Renewed Hearts, Renewed Church
The Crossroads Publishing Co., 1995
(out of print)

One Heart at a Time: Renewing the Church in the New Millennium
Sophronismos Press, 1999

Sunday Nights: Encouraging Words for Young Adults
Sophronismos Press, 2000
(out of print)

Diocesan Priests in the Archdiocese of Louisville
Archdiocese of Louisville Vocation Office, 2001

Religious Communities in the Archdiocese of Louisville
Archdiocese of Louisville Vocation Office, 2002

For the Record: Encouraging Words for Ordinary Catholics
Sophronismos Press, 2003

Intentional Presbyterates: Claiming Our Common Sense of
Purpose as Diocesan Priests
Sophronismos Press, 2003

For the Record II: More Encouraging Words for Ordinary Catholics
Sophronismos Press, 2004

From Seminarian to Diocesan Priest: Managing a Successful
Transition
Sophronismos Press, 2004

Copies of Father Knott's books can be ordered via e-mail by
sending a request to: scholarshop@saintmeinrad.edu.

FOR THE RECORD III

Still More ...
Encouraging Words for Ordinary Catholics

J. Ronald Knott

Sophronismos Press   Louisville, Kentucky

FOR THE RECORD III
Still More ... Encouraging Words for Ordinary Catholics

First Printing: October 2005
ISBN 0-9668969-6-3

Printed in the United States of America

Morris Publishing
3212 East Highway 30
Kearney, NE 68847
1-800-650-7888

To the many ordinary Catholics whose enduring faith has kept me in the priesthood for more than thirty-five years and made it the joy of my life.

ACKNOWLEDGMENTS

I would like to thank Mr. Joseph Duerr, editor of The Record, our archdiocesan newspaper, for giving me the opportunity to write these weekly columns. I also thank Mr. Glenn Rutherford for editing these columns each week and for giving me valuable advice along the way. I would like to offer a special thanks to Ms. Lori Massey for further editing and also formatting these columns into a book. Last of all, I would like to thank the many, many people who have responded so favorably to these columns each week.

"Encourage one another."

II Corinthians 13:11

Onward to a Fourth Year of Columns

You have followed my teaching, way of life, purpose, faith, patience, love and endurance. 2 Timothy 3:10

I cannot believe it, but with this column, I have finished my third year of writing "An Encouraging Word." When I started on Sept. 26, 2002, I had decided that I could write a few encouraging words to ordinary Catholics who were suffering from the fall-out of the sexual abuse scandal. I did not consider how long I would do it.

I have been challenged by this opportunity. It has been more work and took a lot more personal discipline than I ever imagined. It seems the deadline hounds have always been barking on the horizon. Writing something every week means that I have had to do a lot of inner searching. It has been good for me, but it has also meant that I have spent a lot of holidays and evenings writing, just to keep up.

I have been humbled by this opportunity, as well. Wherever I go around the diocese, be it parishes in the city or country, whether it is grocery stores or restaurants, I have run into strangers, from farmers to professionals, who know me from this column. They tell me how much they look forward to it and how much it helps them. These columns have been clipped and mailed all over the country.

The American writer, Jessamyn West, once said, "Talent is helpful in writing, but guts are absolutely necessary." I could not agree more. Baring your soul and sharing your spiritual insights is risky business. When you lay your soul bare for the masses, you are bound to invite attacks.

I have learned much writing these columns. I have learned that words are powerful, that what I want to say is not always what is heard. There have been times when a negative letter to the editor has shocked and surprised me, whether it came from a fellow priest, an unknown parishioner or even a nursing home administrator.

I have learned that I have a choice in light of negative criticism. I can be so careful not to offend that I end up with something so vanilla, so harmless, so spiceless, that nobody would want to read it.

I will, therefore, continue to stick my skinny little neck out there. Since it seems to be good for me and most people have enjoyed reading it, I will try it for a fourth year.

Let me end this third year not with overwhelming confidence, but with a few of my favorite quotes.

Abraham Maslow said:

"It seems the necessary thing to do is not to fear mistakes, to plunge in, to do the best that one can, hoping to learn enough from blunders to correct them eventually."

Ralph Waldo Emerson said:

"God will not have his work made manifest by cowards."

T.S. Eliot said:

"Only those who risk going too far can possibly find out how far they can go."

September 29, 2005

Table of Contents

Preface: Onward to a Fourth Year of Columns v

You Really Can't Take it With You 1

Building on a Firm Foundation of Faith 3

CSA: A Time to be More, Not Less, Generous 5

The Problems with "Sweating the Small Stuff" 7

The Reality of "Telling All" in Public 9

Priests Should be Real, Holy and Effective 11

The Undervalued Contribution of Women 13

Appreciating Our Weekly "Thanksgiving" Meal 15

Today's Seminarians are an Impressive Lot 17

The Problems of the "Priest Shortage" 19

At Nord's Bakery, People "Shine Like the Sun" 21

May the Love of God Shine Through for You 23

Opening our Hearts to New Beginnings 25

The Truth about Negative Religion: It Sells! 27

Coping with Seasonal Affective Disorder 29

A Word about the World of Writing 31

Praying to God to Help us do What He Wants 33

Don't be a Phony When it Comes to Fasting 35

Remember: We are Called to "Give Alms" 37

Finding the Path to Holiness 39

We Each Have a Specific Path to Walk 41

We are Called to Make a Difference 43

The Eucharist: Handed to us from God 45

Change Never Comes Without a Price 47

Change Often Calls for a New Way of Thinking 49

Some Observations about Observing Humans 51

Milking Life for All It's Worth 53

Our Stomachs are Full; Our Hearts are Empty 55

Should we Lower our Standards or Try Harder? 57

Thirty-Five Years as a Priest 59

Some "Snapshots" of the Early Church 61

Dealing with Critics of the Church 63

Doubt is not the Opposite of Faith 65

Staying Connected with God 67

What We Need are Conversions, not Crusades 69

Some Good Things that Get Little Attention 71

Loving the Sinner while Hating the Sin 73

Deacons and their Wives Often Unappreciated 75

Sometimes It's Hard to Keep on Caring 77

The People of Small Parishes are Special 79

Pray to Keep the Priests we Have 81

Faith is a Garden that Needs Regular Attention 83

A New Place with a New View of the World 85

Cell Phone Use Could Be a Sign of Loneliness 87

Coming to Terms with our Personal Histories 89

"All Are Welcome! All Are Welcome!" 91

Sometimes We Already Know the Answer 93

Growing the Seeds God Planted In Us 95

Keeping Faith in the Church 97

You Really Can't Take it With You

You fool, this night your life will be demanded of you; and the things you have prepared, to whom will they belong? Luke 12.

Woody Allen once said, "I know everyone dies, but I am still hoping an exception will be made in my case."

Like all humor, there is a bit of truth in that line. It seems that the possibility of our own death is something that has to be forced into our consciousness.

When we are healthy — and especially when we are young — our own death is merely a concept. It takes a major illness or surviving a tragic accident to bring the reality of our own death home to us. Until that point we proceed as if we were going to live forever, accumulating and saving until the day when we can say to ourselves, "Now I have enough stored up; I can finally rest, eat, drink and be merry." Then "bam," a sudden heart attack or fatal accident and it's over, with all that saved-up stuff going to someone else.

One of the saddest documentaries I have ever seen on TV was one about the wealthy, lonely widows in Florida. It seems that their husbands had obsessively and compulsively worked their whole lives, trying to get to that magic day when they could retire and "enjoy life," only to die of an unforeseen heart attack before they got there.

I am reminded of a joke I once heard about two old ladies standing at the casket of an extremely wealthy old lady friend who had just passed away. One woman whispered to the other, "How much money do you think she left?" The other once whispered back, "All of it, I would guess."

Jesus teaches us that money, while being a necessary thing in life, is unreliable for real security. Thieves can steal it; we can lose it; it can create distance between ourselves and others. But most importantly, we can't take it with us when we die. Jesus teaches us not to obsess about storing material treasures for ourselves that are here today and gone tomorrow, but to strive to be rich in the things that matter to God.

It is important to understand that Jesus was not saying money is evil, but rather that all-consuming love and trust of money is the root of evil. The love and trust of money, the obsessive pursuit of material possessions, puts relationships with others and God way down at the bottom of the list. When "making a living" becomes more important than "living," our happiness is on a slippery slope.

What is the point of obsessively driving ourselves to "have more" if it ruins our health, destroys our marriages and strains our friendships? What is the point of "gaining the whole world" if it drives a wedge between ourselves and our neighbors, makes us intolerably irritable to be around and turns our children into resentful strangers in their own homes?

October 7, 2004

Building on a Firm Foundation of Faith

Which of you wishing to construct a tower does not first sit down and calculate the cost? Otherwise, after laying the foundation, may find himself unable to finish the work. Luke 14

Like every priest I know these days, I have more than one job. One of my jobs involves celebrating Eucharist at Bellarmine University every weekend and on several special occasions throughout the year, including convocations and baccalaureates. Over the last six years, I have written and delivered more than 270 homilies at Bellarmine alone. I don't have to do this, but I choose to do it. I do it because I want to help these Catholic young adults build a solid foundation under their childhood faith, to help them make the transition from an inherited faith to a freely-chosen adult faith. It is my hope that this solid foundation will serve them well as professionals, marriage partners, parents and contributing members of their parishes.

In the Gospel passage above, Jesus talks about the necessity of building our discipleship on a solid foundation and having the resources to finish the project. It's easy to claim discipleship, but it takes courage, fortitude and sacrifice to carry through, day in and day out.

Only an idiot would set out to build a tower with only enough money to dig a foundation. Only a fool would go to war against 20,000 troops with 10,000 troops. In the same way, it would be crazy for young adults who want to be serious disciples of Jesus to go into today's world without a solid spiritual foundation.

Young adulthood is the time when young Catholics will either choose to keep their Catholic faith and go deeper into it, or they will lose it to a slow death by starvation. No one, not even their parents, can make them choose. It is their call.

In the next few years, most of them will have careers, get married and become parents. Without a solid spiritual foundation, their personal faith, their careers, their marriages and their children could be adversely affected by the storms and high winds that will lash against them and shake their very foundations.

Without the firm foundation that a solid faith can offer, they could end up losing their religious heritage, end up in divorce, see their children ruined and their careers destroyed by hostile forces from the outside and personal weakness on the inside. A solid spiritual foundation is the best insurance against the destructive forces that will lash against them in the years to come. A firm religious foundation is my hope for them and why I choose to be there for them.

No matter how tired I am on Sunday nights, no matter how many Masses I have celebrated that weekend, my energy level picks up as soon as I see them coming down from the parking lot or up from the dorms. I am impressed by their attention and reverence at Mass. My own faith is strengthened as I pray with them.

October 14, 2004

CSA: A Time to be More, Not Less, Generous

Tell them to do good, to be rich in good works, to be generous and ready to share.
1 Timothy 6:18

I upped my Catholic Services Appeal gift by 25 percent this year.

Before you jump to the conclusion that I have been put up to this by the CSA campaign staff, let me tell you right off the bat that this is an unsolicited testimonial. They don't even know I am writing this column.

I upped my gift this year to express my gratitude. I am a happy priest again, after a big slump, and I am truly thankful. It has been a practice of mine for many years to share a little extra with others when I am blessed. This little burst of generosity comes from a grateful heart.

Most Catholics have generously continued to support the many ministries funded by CSA, in good times and in bad. Angry, disappointed and frustrated, there are some who have refused, or will refuse, to give to the CSA as a way to punish "the Church." My hope is that they will not punish "the church" just because they want to punish "the Church."

When people talk about "the Church," they usually mean the hierarchy. When people talk about "the church," they usually mean "the people" of the church. Boycotting the CSA will not hurt "the Church" nearly as much as it will hurt "the church." The CSA funds religious, educational and social service programs throughout the archdiocese: emergency assistance to the poor, school counseling programs, lay ministry training and direct services to parishes, to name a few.

5

Boycotting the CSA will hurt the poor, children, lay ministers and our ability to do the work of Jesus in this community.

Over the years, the people I have served have been helped by CSA. In the "home missions" we received help from CSA. When I was a pastor, I sent many people to the various agencies for training, counseling and assistance. As campus ministers, we receive help in our outreach to Catholic young adults. As the vocation director, I received help from CSA to pay for the training of our new priests.

With an office in the Maloney Center, every day I saw the good that CSA does through the many agencies housed there: multicultural ministries, ministry to the deaf, liturgical ministries, Catholic television, diaconate ministry, and marriage and family ministry, to name a few. Even this column is brought to you with help from the CSA.

These last two years been a rough two years for the church and everyone in it, but we are recovering. As we continue to recover from our recent woes, we need to be more generous, not less generous. The church will "get well" not by us withholding assistance, but by us offering assistance. This assistance includes some of our time, a share of our talents and part of our treasure.

Finally, we all need to speak "an encouraging word" to each other and get on with being the Body of Christ in the world.

October 21, 2004

The Problems with "Sweating the Small Stuff"

I do not run as a man who loses sight of the finish line. 1 Corinthians 9:26

Most people today live lives that are intense and complicated. It is easy to get lost. It is common to become overwhelmed and forget why we do what we do.

When we take our eyes off the finish line, our goal, we begin to make the accidentals essential and the essentials accidental. We end up "sweating the small stuff."

We are a country of overworked people. "Making a living" has now become more important than "living." The stress of "the rat race" is taking its toll on marriages, families and professions. Divorce, tranquilizing drug abuse, stress-related heart attacks, parental neglect and accidents from "road rage" are commonplace.

Priests are not immune. Most priests have more than one ministry. Parishes are getting more complicated. There are staffs to hire and manage. There are funds to be raised and protected. There are buildings to be built and managed. There are people to see and meetings to attend.

There are multiple Masses to be celebrated, weddings to witness, people to be buried, fights to be refereed and babies to be baptized. There are meals to be cooked, prayers to be said, friendships to be maintained, books to be read and their own families to be visited.

Even our church can get bogged down in the details while the "big stuff" goes unattended. A few weeks ago I complained about our recent obsession with liturgical minutiae while our members go spiritually unfed, wars rage and violence mushrooms. I suppose, if you feel powerless over the "big stuff," sweating over the small stuff is a good way to feel like you have some control. I find it distracting.

Those who are trying to raise a family and maintain a marriage need to stop every once in a while to remember who is important and why they do what they do. Priests need to stop every once in a while and remember what is truly important and why they do what they do. Our church would benefit by raising its eyes off insignificant details and remembering that announcing the "good news" of God's universal and unconditional love is really the bottom line.

Several years back, I chose the story of Peter's walk on water as the Gospel reading for my 25th anniversary celebration. It both described my first 25 years and offered a pattern for me to follow in my remaining years. As long as Peter kept his eyes fixed on Jesus, he was able to walk on water. It was only when he took his eyes off Jesus and noticed how deep the water was, and how high the winds were, that he began to sink.

The same goes for us. When we take our eyes off the finish line, forget what is truly important, focus on the distractions, we "go under." Maybe the best thing we can do for ourselves these days is to stop and remember why we are doing what we are doing.

October 28, 2004

The Reality of "Telling All" in Public

We even boast of our afflictions, knowing
that affliction produces endurance, and
endurance proven character, and proven
character, hope. Romans 4:3, 4

I have a New York Times cartoon thumb-tacked on the wall near my computer where I do my writing. It pictures a young lady, sitting comfortably in a window sill, a cup of tea at her side, with a note pad on her raised knees. The caption reads, "Dear Mom and Dad: Thanks for the happy childhood. You've destroyed any chance I had of becoming a great writer."

It made me realize again that if things had not been the way they were when I was young, I would probably not have anything to preach or write about today. Some people have warned me that it is dangerous to be so open about my wounds. But, for the most part, I have ignored them and spilled my guts, not just as a cheap way to get sympathy, but whenever I think it might be helpful to others.

There is one caution to "telling all" in a public way. Above the cartoon mentioned above, I also have a quote from a late baseball player named Johnny Sain. He says, "People don't want to hear about the labor pains. They just want to see the baby."

Just spilling your guts in public is intrusive and doesn't help people, unless you can show that you have gone through some healing and triumphed over your problem. People want to see a positive outcome, or else you are dismissed as whining.

"Voyeur television" started with "Candid Camera." Now we have one "reality" show after another where people tell all, knowingly or unknowingly. The guests on Jerry Springer merely expose their wounds for voyeurs to laugh at. At least the guests on "Dr. Phil" and "Oprah Winfrey" expose their wounds to get help and to help others heal.

St. Paul bragged often about his "woundedness." When speaking of his mysterious "thorn in the flesh," he brags about his "weaknesses, insults, hardships, persecutions and constraints," not in some sick, narcissistic way to get sympathy and attention, but "for the sake of Christ." He believed that "when I am weak, then I am strong."

In our relationships with others, it is often our victory over pain and suffering, not just how much we suffered, that can be helpful to those who are experiencing their own pain and suffering. Talking about how good we have it, how lucky we have been and how clever we are usually turns people off.

What I am talking about here is "compassion," a Latin word meaning "to suffer with." The dictionary defines "compassion" as "deep awareness of the suffering of another coupled with the wish to relieve it."

When I "spill my guts" and "tell my story" in these columns, it is not to get sympathy, but to be a "wounded healer."

November 4, 2004

Priests Should be Real, Holy and Effective

The lost I will seek out, the strayed I will bring back, the injured I will bind up and the sick I will heal, shepherding them rightly.
Ezekiel 34:14,16

I have been in a position, especially since I came to Louisville, to hear from a broad range of Catholics about what they want from their priests. I got "an ear full" when I specialized in returning Catholics at the Cathedral of the Assumption. The same was true when I preached in more than 100 of our parishes as a vocation director and when I preached to more than 55 parish missions directed to discouraged and alienated Catholics.

Before I begin to summarize what I have heard, let me summarize what the church says about priests. The church says that priests have three roles: preachers of the Word, presiders at the sacraments and leaders of the community. Those of us who are "diocesan priests" rather than "religious order" priests are called from the laity, to live among the laity, so as to serve and empower the laity.

Preaching, according to Vatican II, is our "primary duty." Good preaching is the one thing I hear lay people say they crave most of all, but don't get enough of, from their priests. As Father Eugene Hemrick, another regular columnist in this paper, said recently, "To strengthen confidence, the church needs outstanding, energetic persons (like Pope John Paul II and Bishop Sheen) blessed with the talent of knowing the culture and being able to address it in a way that connects with people."

Presiding at the sacraments is the thing that most priests say they like doing the most. A growing number of young priests say they prefer to be "cultic" priests rather than "servant leader" priests. Along with quality of preaching, I believe lay people want quality presiding as well as quality music.

They want neither constant, idiotic experimentation nor slavish ritualism. I would summarize their wants in this area as "doing well what is in the book," including the options. They want the sacraments celebrated with heart, but without excessive personalism or unfeeling formality.

In the community, priests are leaders — not the only leaders, but leaders nonetheless. My sense is that people are weary of immaturity, bad service, incompetence and the inability to lead. Lay people today want, expect and deserve competent pastors with the ability to elicit from and coordinate the gifts of lay people.

Lay people want priests to lead, but they want them to avoid the extremes of authoritarianism and abdication. Authoritarianism dismisses the rightful role of others as also responsible for carrying out Christ's work.

Abdication of leadership is equally destructive. Some priests have assumed that encouraging lay ministry means the abdication of their pastoral authority. When they do, all kinds of craziness fills the vacuum.

In short, lay people want their priests to be real, holy and effective; to be good and good at what they do.

November 11, 2004

The Undervalued Contribution of Women

The twelve accompanied him, and also some women: Mary called the Magdalen, Joanna, the wife of Herod's steward Chuza, Susanna, and many others who were assisting them out of their means. Luke 8:1-3

It has been said that "a little knowledge is a dangerous thing." This is certainly true of the immensely popular novel, The Da Vinci Code. It is a novel (emphasis on novel) spun from a few very basic facts into an engaging story that is based more on wishful thinking than on reality. The "facts" upon which the author bases his story are really very slim. Some of the "facts" are simply created to make a case.

The facts are: we don't know very much about the role of women in the early church, and the church has seriously undervalued, and still does, the contribution of women. From these two facts, the author spins a story about "secret" gospels and a church conspiracy theory. If people understand it is only as novel, that's fine, but they really need to know that the facts on which this novel is based are very slim indeed.

The reason for its popularity is certainly more important than the novel itself. It seems that whenever there is a vacuum, there is also a need to fill it, sometimes even with entertaining novels. If the church continues undervaluing the contribution of women, these kinds of "answers" will continue to fill the void.

The explosion of lay ministry in our church has largely been the story of lay women taking on roles that were once reserved for nuns and priests. Of the 35,000 lay ministers currently working in parishes,

80 percent are women, and their numbers are booming. Some are even leading parishes. This is not just some nice thing we "let them do." We need them.

Unless we wake up and quit taking the contributions of women for granted, over-utilizing while at the same time undervaluing them, we could lose some of our most loyal workers. Sixty-eight percent of Catholic women in 1987 said they would never leave the church. That dropped to 65 percent in 1993 and to 56 percent in 1999. We may be reaching a tipping point when it comes to the loyalty of our most reliable core membership.

In light of their great devotion to the church, not to mention our pressing need for their ministry, Catholic women deserve our respect, appreciation and encouragement, at the very time we need to encourage them the most. There are those who are not looking for ways to include them more, but for ways to take back from them the progress they have made. If this continues, we do it to our peril.

If we continue down this path of not supporting and encouraging the ministry of women, who do the lion's share of the work, taking their contributions for granted, we should not be surprised if more drift away.

November 18, 2004

Appreciating Our Weekly "Thanksgiving" Meal

Give thanks to the Lord for he is good, for his kindness endures forever. 1 Chronicles 16:34

I cringe when I hear people say that they don't go to Mass at this or that parish because they don't "get anything out of it." Is it not enough that Jesus is "made present" in word and sacrament at every Mass, no matter how dull the priest is or how awful the music?

When people say they didn't "get anything out of it," they usually mean they didn't get an engaging homily or uplifting music. What they want to get is a new insight and maybe a warm feeling. While these things are good in themselves, "getting something" is not our real purpose for being there.

If we don't "get anything out of it," it is probably because we didn't "bring anything to it."

The word "Eucharist" means "to give thanks." When we gather for the Eucharist, we gather primarily not to get something but to give something. We gather to give thanks for what we have already been given.

We may do a better job giving thanks at our family thanksgiving table than we do at our parish thanksgiving table. If only we could bring the spirit of Thanksgiving Day to churches. On Thanksgiving Day, we gather with our families around a table breaking down with goodness. Spoken or not, a feeling of gratitude and appreciation pervades our civil holiday of Thanksgiving. We give thanks for how full our cup is: plenty of food, more clothes than we need and family ties.

When we gather on Sundays for our spiritual thanksgiving meal, we gather around a table breaking down with goodness, but too often we complain about how empty our cup is: the homily is not interesting, the music is poor, the church is too hot or cold, the priest is taking too long.

Priests can certainly do a better job at presiding and preaching, and lectors and musicians can do a better job at performing their ministries. But the fact remains that all of us can do a better job at counting our blessings before we get there so that we can give thanks no matter how poorly others do their job.

I am always amazed at the faith of those who have to celebrate the Eucharist in desperate situations, how much it means to them and the risk they take to celebrate it. We have all heard of priests celebrating the Eucharist clandestinely in some prison camp, risking life and limb to acquire a pinch of bread and a few drops of wine to celebrate the Eucharist. You would never hear them complain that they didn't "get anything out of it."

Maybe a bigger problem than poor homilies and bad music is the lack of faith among believers. When the congregation's faith is weak, it is more likely for the people in it to demand that others make the Eucharist more meaningful for them.

November 25, 2004

Today's Seminarians are an Impressive Lot

On seeing them, Paul gave thanks to God and took courage. Acts 18:15

Well, I'm back in the seminary again. Maybe I'll get it right this time. As a seminarian, I did not shine, especially during the during the first years. I wasn't on anybody's "most likely to succeed" list. I never graduated with honors. Now I'm back in the seminary again, this time as a teacher, learning all over again.

Every once in a while I have to laugh to myself: "If this place would hire me, it has either sunk to an all-time low or I have grown a lot since the last time I was here." I like to think it's the latter.

Living in the seminary with seminarians is very different from being their vocation director. As vocation director, you know them more from files and evaluations than through interaction and observation. Living with them, praying with them, eating with them and playing with them, you start getting a clearer picture of the quality of our future priests.

I am impressed. They seem to be well-balanced, fun, funny and fun-loving. They are talented, smart, prayerful, generous, healthy and intense. They seem to be more serious about their formation than we were, often going beyond what is required.

In many ways they are like we were. In other ways they are very different. Like us, they are products of their upbringing, but here is the difference. We grew up in the very structured world of the 1940s and '50s and in a pre-Vatican II church where we were told what to do and how to think.

We craved freedom. They have grown up in a chaotic world of divorce, free love, hyper-individuality and a church in crisis. They crave order.

In their search for personal stability and church order, they tend to be more "conservative." Some believe that it is up to their generation to "save the church" from further chaos and disintegration. They are reaching back and reclaiming some of the old religious forms and symbols that our generation all but discarded.

My hope for them is that, in their search, they will not settle for a mere "restoration," but will choose "transformation." Restoration is about bringing old things back. Transformation is about people changing. They may be the generation that will "bring forth from our storeroom things new and old," putting them together in a new paradigm.

The monks are certainly dedicated to their work of supplying the church with good priests. Good liturgy and examples of fine preaching are modeled daily. These monks are assisted by a faculty of faith-filled, talented men and women, lay, professed and ordained. Father Bernie Lutz and I offer them the perspective and experience of diocesan priesthood.

All of them have made difficult "counter-cultural" decisions, choosing "the road less traveled." A little older than we were, many of them have lived and worked in the real world, holding jobs and living on their own. To me, they are heroes for trying.

December 2, 2004

The Problems of the "Priest Shortage"

Barnabas encouraged them to remain
faithful to the Lord in firmness of heart.
Acts 11:23

I was born in St. Theresa parish in Rhodelia, Kentucky, and I was
pastor of Holy Name of Mary parish in Calvary, Kentucky. Both
parishes are similar in size, make-up and history.

Holy Name of Mary was founded in 1798, and St. Theresa was
founded in 1818. Both have a long Catholic history that goes all the
way back to the earliest settlers on the Kentucky frontier. Both have
about 200 registered households. Sadly, both have, for the first time
in their long histories, joined a growing list of small parishes that no
longer have resident priests.

Even though both are generously served by capable priests from
nearby parishes, it breaks my heart to watch the "domino effect" of
today's priest shortage. It's bad enough when it happens every few
blocks here in the city, but it is especially tragic when it happens to
small, Catholic communities in the rural parts of our archdiocese.

Caught between a rock and a hard place, I believe the archdiocese
is doing its best to deal with this unwelcome reality, but that brings
little comfort to those who are especially feeling the pinch out in the
state.

Thank God that capable lay people, assisted by a growing pool of
deacons, are stepping up to the plate to fill their rightful roles as leaders in the church. But we still need priests. I agree with Pope John
Paul II when he said that the more lay ministry develops, the more we
need holy and effective priests.

As the number of priests shrinks, the number of Catholics is growing. As the number of Catholics grows, the more need there is for the celebration of the Eucharist. For that, we need priests. The Catholic church cannot be strong if the Eucharist is regularly denied because of a lack of priests.

What is the answer? Some are holding out for the tides to turn, waiting until an all-male, celibate clergy becomes popular again. Others are waiting for Rome to change its mind and open priesthood to married men and to women. From what I see and hear, I wouldn't hold my breath in either regard. I can't see either change in the near future.

I have always believed in the axiom that "a breakdown is a sure sign of a breakthrough." I don't have the foggiest idea how all this will shake out, but I do believe that somehow and in some way, the Holy Spirit is working this out as we speak.

In the absence of answers, we can remain faithful. We can keep calling lay people to step forward and share their gifts. Parishes can learn to share resources and ministries. Priests can continue to focus their efforts on the essentials of priesthood. Pulling together in hard times has a way of making us all stronger in the long run.

December 9, 2004

At Nord's Bakery, People "Shine Like the Sun"

I myself am convinced about you, my brothers and sisters, that you are full of goodness. Romans 15:14

As I have written before, I love going to Nord's Bakery on Preston Street. I have been going there so long now that I feel free to jump in and help sack doughnuts and pour coffee when the traffic at the counter gets out of hand.

This has caused more than a few people to be caught off-guard. "Hey, I know you. Aren't you, uh, uh, uh, Father Knott? What are you doing back there?"

Yes, the doughnuts are to die for and the coffee is hot, but that's not the main reason I like to hang out there. I like the people who own it and the people who frequent it.

One day a few weeks ago, it was packed. People were noisily and comfortably interacting. Mike and Lynn Nord were taking orders as fast as they could without denying each customer a big dose of hospitality. It's a family place, so Mike's father and mother, Ken and Ellen, were weaving in and out, offering assistance. Sometimes it's Mary, Joanie or Derek.

When I came through the door, one of the kids who waits for the bus at a nearby stop rushed toward me and hugged me around the legs, as if I was some long-lost relative. I passed Franciscan Brother Ray on his way out the door, hugging a huge box of yesterday's doughnuts to take to the shelter for the poor.

John, Stanley and Mark, who do construction work, were already there with a new Mexican helper. I teased Stanley about seeing him in front of my house the day before, assisting a stranded female motorist. Cliff, the motorcycle shop owner and another regular, arrived.

Back in the corner other regulars, Mabel, Joann and their friends, had staked out a table to celebrate Mabel's 90th birthday. She grew up in Meade County, as I did, and knew some of my family.

There were people coming from early Mass at several surrounding parishes. There were policemen, garbage truck drivers and lawyers. There were students from U of L and retirees from all around.

In a half-hour span, I was updated on the condition of three people with cancer, two with Alzheimer's and one with a botched hip replacement. I heard how the third grade was going and how a couple of building projects were coming along. As a backdrop to all this, I could see the big blackboard with its fitting inspirational quote of the month. It was from Eleanor Roosevelt: "We must do the thing we cannot do."

In spite of all the problems these people are facing, they laughed and shared their troubles with compassionate friends and neighbors. It was amazing to watch. I was suddenly reminded of Thomas Merton's experience at the corner of Fourth and Walnut, about which he wrote, "I was suddenly overwhelmed with the realization that I loved these people," and "There is no way of convincing people that they are walking around shining like the sun."

December 16, 2004

May the Love of God Shine Through for You

Upon those who dwelt in the land of gloom a light has shone. Isaiah 9:1

When I started writing this column more than two years ago, I chose the title "An Encouraging Word" because I wanted to offer a little hope to those who were struggling, especially those who found themselves struggling with the fallout of the "sexual abuse scandal" that exploded from secrecy into broad daylight.

If the truth be known, the writing itself gave me a way to work through my own depression and keep myself hopeful. The fact that it has helped others has been icing on the cake.

In this year's Christmas column, my third, I want to offer "an encouraging word" to those who dread the holidays because of sickness, sadness or loss. Like many priests with whom people share their pain, I am very aware that Christmas is not "jingle bells all the way" for everybody out there.

First, I would like to send "an encouraging word" to those who live alone, especially the elderly who have outlived most of their families and friends. As a priest, I have known what it is like to go back to an empty house or apartment alone, after Mass, when families go home together. I remember more than one Christmas when I went to bed just so I wouldn't have to feel the loneliness.

Second, I would like to send "an encouraging word" to those of you who are dealing with the uncertainty and pain of serious health problems, either personally, in your family or among your close friends. I know several people who are facing cancer, Alzheimer's or other chronic diseases. These things affect not just those who have them, but everyone around them. It is a time of testing: of one's patience, faith and even resources.

Third, I would like to send "an encouraging word" to those who have lost loved ones this year. Even though my mother died 28 years ago, I still get choked up at midnight Mass when I pause "to remember those who have gone before us." Those of you who have lost spouses, children, siblings or close friends this year, especially under tragic situations, will find this Christmas especially painful.

Last, I would like to send "an encouraging word" to the man who writes me from prison, the young woman who is grieving over the loss of a relationship, the children of addicted parents or struggling, divorced, single parents.

That first Christmas was certainly a day of promise, but it was also a day of pain. Mary and Joseph were away from home. Jesus was born in a barn. Herod was out to kill the newborn Jesus.

But, in spite of it all and behind all the details, the incredible love God has for us has shone through. So, no matter what you are facing this Christmas, may the incredible love God has for you shine through. May you know it. May you feel it.

December 23, 2004

Opening our Hearts to New Beginnings

Start it on its way and let it go. Then watch! 1 Samuel 6:8

One of the basic requirements of being a diocesan priest is availability. Moving regularly is built in to our way of life. Every few years, we are required to leave the people and places we know, move into a new, unfamiliar community and begin adjusting all over again.

The whole idea behind celibacy is its potential to free a priest for complete availability to do full-time pastoral service. For example, it is easier to move a celibate, when ministry calls for it, than it is a married man with a family. No matter how rational it sounds in theory, it is still hard to pull up stakes every few years and start all over.

As we enter yet another "new year," most of us have a sense of making a new beginning. I am still trying to adjust to my new job at Saint Meinrad Seminary, with its new eating and sleeping patterns, new relationships and new living conditions.

All new beginnings are filled with hope on one hand and fear on the other. I have bounced back and forth between these two poles ever since I began my new job. I have been dreaming for years about how we could meet the pressing need to give newly ordained priests more help and direction as they come out of the seminary. When the opportunity came to "put up or shut up," I jumped at the chance to create what we now call "The Institute for Priests and Presbyterates."

"Be careful what you pray for, because you may get it," someone once said. At some point last summer, when the reality of what I have gotten myself into hit me, I had a strange dream, as I often do at times like this.

I dreamed I was the last one getting off a bus, when I noticed an abandoned baby stuck in the steering wheel. It didn't cry. It was bluish, sickly and had big bright eyes that locked onto me. Since I was the only one around, I picked it up. I began to ask myself, "How in the world will I ever be able to take care of this baby while trying to do my work as a priest?"

As the dream went on, I remember slowly falling in love with this struggling new life and thinking of ways I could work out the problems it brought. With those big eyes looking at me, I knew I was destined to raise this "baby," problems or not. Where there's a will, there's a way.

Now that my project has been generously funded by the Lilly Foundation, I am committed to stand up to my fears and raise this "baby," one way or another.

That's what all new beginnings are about: the courage to live in hope, stand up to our fears and open our arms to all the "new" that God wants to give us.

January 13, 2005

The Truth about Negative Religion: It Sells!

> I write these few words to encourage you never to let go of the true grace of God to which I bear witness. 1 Peter 5:12

Negativity sells! If you don't believe me, just sit in front of your television and flip through the channels. Murder, scandal, rape, destruction, assault, theft, infidelity, deceit and torture are a few of the subjects that bombard us daily on network and cable TV. That does not even cover "reality" programs, where personal humiliation is a common thread.

We can blame "those Hollywood people" all we want, but the real reason there is so much of it on TV is because it sells, and it sells because people want it.

Negative religion also sells. In general, I find most religious programming embarrassing. If it's not doom and gloom and hysterical, it's syrupy, simplistic and corny.

If I wanted to make money preaching on TV, really big money, I would "go negative," too. I would search the Scriptures for the most obscure apocalyptic passages — you know, those scary, impending hellfire and brimstone passages. I would persuade my audience that God had personally instructed me as to their precise meaning.

I would make dire predictions about the future. I would divide people into two groups: sinners and saints. I would sanctimoniously put myself and those who agree with me in with the "saints" and everybody else in with the "sinners."

I would argue the merits of crusades, inquisitions and witch hunts. I would identify a few scapegoat groups to beat up on. I would rant and rave about their sins, especially sins related to sex. The money would roll in. It always does.

But if I really had my own religious TV program, I wouldn't be mean in God's name. I would preach about God's goodness, mercy and unconditional love. I would seek out sinners and talk to them as Jesus talked to them, with respect and kindness. Instead of seeing goodness in some people and evil in others, I would have people recognize that we all need God because there is some evil in the best of people and some goodness in the worst of people.

If I had my own religious program, I would pray that, like Isaiah, I would have "a well-trained tongue so that I might speak a word of encouragement to the weary."

I would pray for healing words, words like those of Julia Cameron: "I wish I could take language and fold it like cool, moist rags. I would lay words on your forehead. I would wrap words on your wrists. 'There, there,' my words would say — or something better. I would murmur, 'Hush' and 'Shh, shh, it's all right.' I would ask them to hold you all night.

"I wish I could take language and daub and soothe and cool where fever blisters and burns, where fever turns yourself against you. I wish I could take language and heal the words that were wounds you have no names for."

January 20, 2005

Coping with Seasonal Affective Disorder

A joyful heart is the health of the body,
but a depressed spirit dries up the bones.
Proverbs 17:22

It's late January, so I thought I would offer a word of encouragement to those who are "about to climb the walls." They could be suffering from something as serious as "clinical depression" or as harmless as "seasonal affective disorder."

Clinical depression is an illness that involves the body, mind and thoughts and affects the way a person eats and sleeps, the way one feels about oneself and the way he or she thinks about things. I am not qualified to write about this disease, though my heart goes out to those who suffer from it.

Clinical depression, which only a qualified doctor can treat, is completely different from that normal, temporary "down" mood caused by life events or grieving that the majority of us suffer from time to time.

Besides the normal and temporary depression that comes from tragedy and loss, we hear a lot these days about the temporary symptoms of that winter "mood disorder" called "seasonal affective disorder," or SAD for short. SAD is a mood disorder associated with depression episodes and related to seasonal variations of light.

SAD was first noted before 1845, but was not officially named until the early 1980s. As seasons change, there is a shift in our "biological internal clocks" due partly to changes in sunlight patterns. This can cause our biological clocks to be out of step with our daily schedules. The most difficult months for SAD sufferers are January and February, and younger persons and women are at higher risk.

So if you are feeling a little down this month, you may not be going crazy after all. It may just be hormonal. The hormone, melatonin, which is produced at increased levels in the dark, has been linked to SAD. Therefore, when the days are shorter and darker, the production of this hormone increases.

Here are a few suggestions. If you can afford it, go to Florida, Hawaii or the Caribbean—anywhere the sun shines. For the majority who cannot afford such luxury, bright light therapy has been shown to suppress the brain's secretion of melatonin. Even though there have been no research findings to definitely link this therapy with an anti-depressant effect, I have noticed several hundred Internet sights selling such equipment.

One study found that an hour's walk in winter sunlight was as effective as two and a half hours under bright artificial light. Either sounds like a healthier option than pressuring your doctor for an anti-depressant.

Maybe the best thing to do in January and February is to eat and sleep less, get more exercise and sunlight, and focus on the needs and problems of others—anything besides "holing up" at home with a wide-screen TV and a barrel of chips, feeling sorry for yourself. For those who enjoy a good "pity party" every winter, as an old country song puts it, "you can feel bad if it makes you feel better."

January 27, 2005

A Word about the World of Writing

The community read it and were delighted with the encouragement it gave them. Acts 15:31

One of the results of writing this column is that people are always sharing copies of things they write with me. This week, I want to offer "an encouraging word" to those of you who have always had a secret desire to try your hand at writing for publication.

When I majored in English in college, I had no idea that I would be a writer. I majored in English on purpose, but ended up being a writer by accident.

Over the years, people have told me that I needed to publish my homilies. I dismissed them as "just being nice," telling them that "if I had an editor," I might think about it. One day, Michael Downey, a former professor at Bellarmine, showed up at the Cathedral. On his way out of church, he too told me that I should think about publishing my homilies. I gave him my standard "I would, if I had an editor" response. He told me that he was an editor for Crossroad Press in New York.

With his help, and with the support of Jeanne Paradis, I published my first book, An Encouraging Word, a collection of Cathedral homilies. It went through two printings and was distributed in several countries. I followed up with a second collection of Cathedral homilies, One Heart at a Time, which I "self-published." A little later, I completed a collection of Bellarmine homilies, entitled Sunday Nights.

As vocation director, I finished two books on religious vocations, Diocesan Priests in the Archdiocese of Louisville and Religious Communities in the Archdiocese of Louisville. Two years ago, I started writing this weekly column and published two collections, entitled For the Record and For the Record II.

All the above books are out of print, except for a reprint of For the Record and the newly completed For the Record II, which are both available through The Record. Any profits from these books go to help our seminarians.

I finished two more books this year for priests and seminarians. More than two thousand copies of Intentional Presbyterates, a book on "team building" among priests, are now being used in dioceses across the country. From Seminarian to Diocesan Priest will be available soon to help fifth-year seminarians in several seminaries make a successful transition into diocesan priesthood.

I would never call myself a great writer, but I have been surprised by people's acceptance of what I have had to say. What I have learned is that our people are starving for some simple, down-to-earth, spiritual encouragement. As long as there is an audience, I will continue to write.

If there are any would-be writers out there who would like to try their hand at "self-publishing," I would be happy to share a few pointers on getting started. You can contact me at jrknott@bellsouth.net. As St. Francis said, "If God can work through me, he can work through anyone."

February 3, 2005

Praying to God to Help us do What He Wants

"May it be done to me according to your word." Luke 1:38

It's Lent. It's time for our traditional, spiritual disciplines of prayer, fasting and almsgiving.

Over the next three weeks, I want to offer some encouragement in each of the three. Today, I want to say a few words about prayer.

I can never write about prayer without thinking of the men I used to talk with before Sunday Mass in front of Holy Name of Mary Church in Calvary, Ky. They were not only wise, they were funny.

Since many of them were farmers, one of the regular subjects of discussion was the weather. "We need rain." "We've had way too much rain." "Do you think it will rain?"

One Sunday, we were theorizing about the weather when the conversation turned to prayer. It didn't take long for someone to suggest that we pray for rain at Mass.

One of the men, a real comedian, told the story about praying for rain a few years back. "You know, Father Knott, it was so dry that we decided to light one of those 30-day candles and pray for rain. Well, it started raining and wouldn't quit. After two weeks, we had to go into church and blow it out."

What is the purpose of prayer?

Many people believe prayer is about buttering up God so that he will give us what we want. In reality, prayer is more about asking God to change us so that we will want what he wants for us. God doesn't need to do the changing; we do.

From all I know about prayer, the best two examples of ideal prayer I can think of are the prayers of Mary, the mother of Jesus, and Solomon, King of Israel. They do not ask God to do what they want. They ask God to help them do what he wants.

After all I have done for you!

February 10, 2005

Don't be a Phony
When it Comes to Fasting

Do not be like the hypocrites. Matthew 6:5

How are your Lenten resolutions of prayer, fasting and almsgiving going?

It's not that hard to do, it's just hard to remember to do it. If you are one of us who has already failed a few times to keep your resolutions, don't give up. You can always begin again.

Last week, I wrote about prayer. This week, I want to write about fasting. Next week, I will write about almsgiving.

Fasting, the partial or total abstinence from food and drink, has been a part of virtually every religion from primitive to modern times. Fasting has been practiced for a variety of reasons: as a means of repentance for sin, as a remembrance of being forgiven for past sins, of supplication in times of disaster, as a way to remember the dead and as a way to prepare oneself for a serious undertaking. Fasting has been understood as a symbolic act of prayer and humility.

In early Christianity, the motive for fasting shifted to an emphasis on bodily discipline. Since people back then believed that evil spirits entered the mouth with food, fasting would help avoid the influences of evil spirits. It was also seen as a way to purify the mind for contemplation and communion with God. Fasting was a major part of Jesus' desert retreat before he started his public ministry. It also was viewed as a way of uniting oneself with the suffering of Christ.

As we learned from the Gospel of Ash Wednesday, when Jesus spoke about these three traditional spiritual practices, he did not say, "If you pray, if you fast or if you give alms," as if it is optional. He assumes these practices are part of our spiritual lives, so he says "when" you pray, fast and give alms. And when you do these things, he says, don't be a hypocrite about it.

The word "hypocrite" is a good Greek word. A "hypocrite" is simply an actor, one who performs on a stage. In our society, however, it is synonymous with a fake or a phony. When it comes to the spiritual discipline of fasting, Jesus simply says, don't just pretend to be fasting; really do it. Don't be a phony about it.

I suppose the perfect example of phony fasting is our habit of replacing cheap meat with expensive seafood. Part of our fasting tradition is the abstention from meat on Ash Wednesday, the Fridays of Lent and Good Friday. Giving up hot dogs and meat loaf during Lent and replacing them with shrimp, lobster, Chilean sea bass and scallops is, in my book, playing games. It may meet the letter of the law, but is certainly is not in the spirit of the law.

If we are going to "do Lent," let's really "do Lent." Let's be serious. Forget frog legs and stuffed flounder; eat that hot dog, bologna sandwich or a cheap box of generic macaroni and cheese. Now, that really hurts.

February 17, 2005

Remember: We are Called to "Give Alms"

When you give alms, do not blow a trumpet
before you to win the praise of others.
God who sees in secret will repay you.
Matthew 6:2,4

Today I want to write about the third of the traditional spiritual disciplines of Lent: almsgiving. Last week and the week before, I wrote about prayer and fasting.

Almsgiving is a religiously motivated giving of money or other resources to benefit those needing them. Often linked to prayer and fasting, it is a prominent feature in several major religions and holds a special place in Jewish and Christian religious practice.

The Hebrew word for alms means both "alms" and "justice," implying that almsgiving restores God's right order, a closing of the gap between the rich and the poor. St. Basil of Caesarea (d. 379) affirmed that the excess wealth of the rich is the property of the poor, and failure to give alms to the poor amounted to theft from them. St. Ambrose of Milan (d. 397) also said that property beyond one's needs belongs by right to those who lack necessities.

Medieval Christians gave their alms to monasteries and cathedral churches because of their ability to organize hospices and food programs for the poor. In the later Middle Ages, the begging orders, such as the Franciscans, were maintained through almsgiving. In contemporary experience, almsgiving has taken the form of personal or organizational support for established charities and an emphasis on addressing the causes of poverty, in addition to alleviating its effects.

To give alms is a tangible way to "love God and one's neighbor as oneself." To give alms is to mimic the self-giving of God himself.

Jesus warned us in the Ash Wednesday Gospel that when we give alms, we should try to do it without drawing attention to ourselves or our gifts. He tells us not to be like those who go to the temple and have trumpets blowing and cameras rolling when they make their donations.

In a day where charitable gifts are tax-deductible and rewarded by plaques, trophies, honorary degrees or even having buildings named after the donor, most of us have grown to expect some notoriety to come with our giving. And some are even offended when their gifts are not recognized in such a way. There is nothing wrong with that, but Jesus says that attention from people will be your only reward. If you want God to reward you, keep it between the two of you.

We are called this Lent to "give alms," to be generous with our assets. Anyone who wants to can come up with a million good excuses to avoid giving away a share of his or her blessings. But I am hopeful that many of us will look, rather, for opportunities to give.

The easiest way to give alms is to support those smart organizations who best know how to help the poor. Personal involvement in such organizations is even better. Of course, there is nothing wrong with spontaneous, anonymous and random acts of generosity. This last is one of my personal favorites.

February 24, 2005

Finding the Path to Holiness

After he had sat down, his disciples came
to him and he began to teach them.
Matthew 5:1-12

What are the traits of a "holy" person? One who bears a title and wears a robe? Not necessarily.

One who lives isolated in a monastery or hermitage? Maybe. One who is able to quote the Bible, chapter and verse? Sometimes.

What are the traits of a holy person? Jesus tells us, very simply, what holiness looks like. He says that a holy person has several qualities.

Blessed are the poor in spirit. People who are holy are first of all people who put their relationships with God and people above everything else in life. They have their priorities straight.

Blessed are they who mourn. People who are holy are not so jaded and self-centered that they no longer have the ability to feel compassion for those who suffer. Holy people are the opposite of cold and heartless people.

Blessed are the meek. People who are holy know their strengths and weaknesses. They neither inflate their worth nor devalue it. "Holy" people have an unpretentious, down-to-earth goodness about them.

Blessed are they who hunger and thirst for righteousness. People who are holy want to get to know God more, want to become better people and are passionate about trying to do what God asks of them. Knowing God and serving God are the central passions of holy people.

Blessed are the merciful. People who are holy give other people a break, the benefit of the doubt, a good hearing, rather than a rush to judgment. They withhold judgment and extend mercy, knowing that they cannot see into other people's hearts.

Blessed are the clean of heart. People who are holy are people who do the right thing and also do it for the right reason. What you see is what you get. Who they appear to be and who they really are match up perfectly.

Blessed are the peacemakers. People who are holy go out and look for opportunities to heal, to reunite, to bring together and to put an end to strife and misunderstanding. They cannot rest until unity and harmony are restored.

Blessed are they who are persecuted. People who are holy are persecuted. Evil cannot bear the presence of goodness. No good deed, or good person for that matter, goes unpunished. The brighter the light, the fiercer the attack. "Holy" people are often hated, abused, persecuted and even killed, simply because they are good.

Blessed are you when they insult and persecute you because of me. People who are holy are not afraid of being known as a friend of God. They do not shove their religion into others' faces, but neither do they hide it.

This kind of person stands in stark contrast to the money-grubbing, cold-hearted, self-inflated, quick-to-judge, self-centered, opportunistic materialist that the world encourages us to be. Lent calls us to examine our lives and to get back on track. The track we are to get back on is the path of discipleship, the path to holiness.

March 3, 2005

We Each Have a Specific Path to Walk

After Jesus was baptized and heard a
voice from heaven, he was led by the Spirit
into the desert. Matthew 3:16,17; 4:1

I believe with all my heart that each one of us has a vocation, a call from God, a specific path to walk in this life. I also believe that if we stay on that path, without wavering from it, that path will not only lead us to ultimate happiness, but walking the path itself brings happiness, that deep-down inner peace that comes from knowing we are on the right path, no matter what life throws at us.

The only problem is finding what our path is and staying on it, without wavering or straying, until our time here is over.

I meet so many people, even in their 30s, 40s and 50s, who do not yet know their path, do not yet know to what they can commit or give their lives. They roam aimlessly from one dead-end street to another, hoping to bump into something to which they can commit.

The Psalmist says, "You will show me the path to life, abounding joy in your presence." Jesus said, "I am the way, the truth and the life. Follow in my footsteps." Even Buddha said, "Our goal in life is to find out what our purpose in life is and to give ourselves to that purpose wholeheartedly."

My path was revealed to me at a very early age. Even though I was only in the second grade, it was unusually clear to me. Even though I knew my path, it was not magic. I had to focus, concentrate, make some hard choices and walk through some hell and high water, not only to get to ordination, but to stay in the priesthood for the last 35 years. It is my intention, and fervent wish, to die walking this path.

In the Gospel story cited above, we are told that Jesus came to his cousin John for baptism. Immediately after his baptism, a voice from heaven told Jesus that he was God's "beloved son." Jesus may have been given the path he was meant to walk, but he needed some clarity on just what being "God's beloved son" meant. We are told that "the Spirit led him into the desert" for a retreat, a time for listening more intently for clarity and direction.

Lent is a time for us to go to "the desert" as well, to get some clarity about our path or to get back on track. It is a time to listen again to our heart of hearts, to say "yes" again to the path that God has given us and "no" to the tempters around us and the tempters in our heads who try to pull us away from where we know we need to go. To do that, you have to spend some quality time with Jesus, some time away from the roar and noise of everyday life.

March 10, 2005

We are Called to Make a Difference

You are the salt of the earth. You are the
light of the world. Matthew 5

You are salt! You are light!

The celebration of baptism is one of the most beautiful, and least understood, ceremonies of the church. Most of the time, young parents, under pressure from their parents, are more eager to "get it done" than to understand its meaning. That's too bad, because baptism has some very powerful, if not well understood, symbols that do what they symbolize.

The main symbol is, of course, water. Water is a powerful symbol because it both gives life and takes it. Water gives life. Ask any farmer. Water also kills. Ask any tsunami survivor.

The waters of baptism give new life and kill sin. That is why the baptism fountain has been called a "womb" and a "tomb."

Historically, the church had two more important symbols taken from this Gospel: salt and light, the symbolic giving of salt and the symbolic giving of a candle. In the old baptismal ritual, after the water was poured over the head of the baby, the priest put a few grains of salt into the baby's mouth with a prayer that he or she would grow up to add some "seasoning" to the world, to make a difference in the world.

After that, the priest hands the parents and godparents a lighted candle, a candle that got its light from that big Easter candle that represents Christ. So in baptism, we all get a small share of Christ's light to take into the world.

Many people, even people who have been through this baptism ceremony, think that their job as a Christian is not to screw up too badly so that they can "go to heaven." Jesus makes the point in today's Gospel that a lamp is not lit to be hidden; it is lit to give light to all in the house. "Just so," he says, "your light must shine before others."

This is especially true of married couples and priests. The catechism says that two of the sacraments are geared toward the salvation of others: marriage and ordination. Contrary to all that has been pumped into us by TV and film, people do not get married for their own good but for the good of their spouses and children.

Likewise, I wasn't ordained for my own good, but for your good. As a diocesan priest, I have been called from the laity, to live among the laity, to serve the laity. My priesthood has no meaning without my relationship to those I serve.

At our baptisms, we accepted our commission to be "salt" and "light" to the world. In baptism, we were called to make a difference in the world. As we come to the conclusion of another Lent, we need to make final preparations to renew our baptismal vows this Easter, vows to be "salt and light" for the good of others.

March 17, 2005

The Eucharist: Handed to us from God

> I received from the Lord what I handed on
> to you, namely Jesus took bread and said,
> "This is my body," a cup saying, "This is
> my blood." 1 Corinthians 11:23

When my grandfather, Leo Knott, died several years ago, my aunt Irma, who was the executrix of his will, gave me his pocket watch. It was "handed on" to me. I feel obliged to "hand it on" to the next generation of Knotts, and since I will have no children, I will be giving it to my brother Gary's son, Wesley, to give to his son, Wesley, Jr.

So when young Wesley gets it, it will have been "handed on to him" from his great- great-grandfather. We are hopeful that he will keep it and "hand it on" to his son and his son's son. It will grow in value as it is passed along.

St. Paul says that the Eucharist was handed to him by the Lord, and he, in turn, was handing it on to the Corinthians. This outline of the Eucharist was written down even before the story of the Last Supper was written in the Gospels a good 15 years later. That means the Eucharist was already being handed down, even before the Gospels were written. People learned about the Eucharist from practice before they learned about it from the written word.

Just think about it. Our weekly gathering in memory of Jesus, around bread and wine, is something that has been "handed down" to us by generation after generation. It was celebrated in Aramaic, Greek and then Latin. Today, it is celebrated in every language on earth. It has been celebrated in great cathedrals and slums, parish churches and prison camps, by the rich and by the poor, by people with deep faith and by people with a careless lack of attention.

I cannot imagine the church without this "source and summit" of the spiritual life. I cannot imagine doing without the Eucharist. I cannot imagine how Catholics could go off and leave it because the organization needs a lot of reform, and some of its leaders have failed. I agree with what Peter said when the people of Jesus' day walked away after he spoke of himself being "the bread of life" and that people should "feed on him." "To whom else shall we go?"

There are a lot of things that need fixing in our church. There are a lot of things that other churches do better than we do. But we have the weekly, even daily, celebration of the Eucharist and that, in my book, trumps all else.

I cannot look at my First Communion picture without remembering how special I felt and how precious I considered what was being "handed on" to me. I was only seven, but rather to turn my back on that gift is unthinkable. I hope to not "drop the ball" but to "hand it on."

March 24, 2005

Change Never Comes Without a Price

Having set out, the Israelite community grumbled against Moses and Aaron, saying, "In the land of Egypt, we sat at our fleshpots and ate our fill of bread, but you lead us into this desert to die of famine." Exodus 16:1-3

When I was a kid in Rhodelia, Ky., we called them "scaredy-cats" and "chickens" — kids who lost their nerve and ran home the first second any kind of bravery was called for.

They were scared to try anything new, anything adventurous, anything out of the ordinary. They were willing to sit around and imagine great adventures. They were willing to make a good start. But they were cowards when it came time to carry through.

The story of the Israelites' exodus out of the slavery of Egypt, across a scary desert to the promised land, is one of my favorites. The people set out behind their leaders, filled with excitement. They assumed that they could get to their new life without having to go through any pain.

When they hit the desert with all its problems, they turned on their leaders and yearned for the good old days, even though those "good old days" were days of slavery. "We might have been in slavery," they said, "but at least we had something to eat."

This story is a paradigm for all people who are undergoing change. There is a part of all of us who want a new life without having to pay any price for it. We want resurrection without the cross. Victims of spouse abuse often get up enough nerve to leave their abusers, only to return to them when they are overwhelmed with fear about not being able to make it on their own.

This "exodus reaction" seems to be a natural human reaction in times of change. When old systems are no longer working or do not fit current experiences, a few individuals — and then great numbers of people — begin to generate unrest and make new proposals. As the unrest grows, those who have a stake in the old culture or who are filled with fear try to summon people back to the old ways.

The people who want to "return to the fleshpots of Egypt," who try to summon people back to the old ways, often have short-term success. Eventually, however, accumulated pressure for change produces such acute stress that the whole culture must break the crust of custom and find new structures.

When that happens, those new proposals become the consensus, and the culture moves into a new age. After a while, even the new way becomes the old way, and the process repeats itself.

In my lifetime, I have seen this dynamic happening in our church. The excitement of Vatican II is now a distant memory. Those who want to "go back" to the days before Vatican II are winning in some places, at least for now. I am not sure where we will go in the next few years, but I am certain we cannot go back.

March 31, 2005

Change Often Calls for a New Way of Thinking

I came into this world so that those who do not see might see. John 9:39

Tyler Perry — African-American playwright, actor and screenwriter — produced and starred in a recent number-one box office hit, "Dairy of a Mad Black Woman." Perry attributes his success to what he calls "spiritual progress," especially, making peace with his own father.

In my estimation, he had a profound insight when he said, "I learned that parents do what they know how." He could have refused to let go of his anger and blame, but he said, "My life changed once things changed in me."

I am amazed when I talk to stuck people. I believe that most people who are stuck are basically people who are blinded by their inability to "see in a new way." They whine and cry and wait to be rescued, but they cannot change their minds and look at their situations from a new angle. They can't let go of their old way of thinking and seeing, and so they remain stuck in their blindness.

They are like the monkeys I read about several years ago. To catch monkeys for the zoo, people would cut a hole in a tree, just small enough for a monkey to stick his hand into. Then they fill the hole with peanuts. When the monkeys stick their hands into the hole and grab the peanuts, they cannot pull their hands back out.

Instead of letting go of the peanuts, monkeys howl and cry till someone comes and hauls them off to the zoo. All they would have to do was to let go of the peanuts. People are a lot like that: they cannot let go of the way they see things and so remain trapped in their suffering. They clutch at beliefs that say life ought to be fair, parents ought to be perfect, spouses should not let each other down, those who lead in the church ought to be perfect, things ought to make sense, and people ought to respect you, love you and meet your needs.

Of course, when it turns out that life isn't fair, when parents and churches aren't perfect, when spouses let each other down, when things don't make sense and when people do not meet their needs, they fall apart and remain stuck in their belief that if they just don't like it enough, it will go away. All they would have to do to free themselves is to let go of their old assumptions and see things in a new way.

Jesus was right when he called for a "metanoia," a new way of seeing and a new way of thinking. Tyler Perry was right on target when he said, "My life changed once things changed in me." When we refuse to change the way we look at things, when things within us resist change, we actually contribute to perpetuating our own suffering.

April 7, 2005

Some Observations about Observing Humans

God looked at everything he had made,
and he found it very good. Genesis 1:31

I like to sit in public places and watch people. I like to observe how people behave and interact with each other and with their environment. I have written several columns from places such as my front porch, a table at a bakery, a chair on the beach and from behind a grocery cart.

Recently, I got the opportunity to sit in the lobby of the hotel in Washington, D.C., where all the bishops of our country hold their annual meeting. I sat there, off and on, watching them come and go and react with each other for two days. I took a lot of notes, but I would not dare put them in a column. Let's just say that it was interesting, very interesting. I found myself being more compassionate.

A few weeks ago, as part of my job, I had to fly to Phoenix by way of Dallas. While I was waiting for planes, I took out my note pad and went into my observer position.

A busy airport is an introvert's worst nightmare. It often appears to be a loud, seething pit of frantic human beings on the edge of a melt-down. On the other hand, maybe it's just me. I like to go places, but I cannot wait to get out of airports wherever I go.

Cheaper fares mean more parents with small kids are traveling. There should be a bravery award for parents who would attempt to travel with several small children. Even though their strollers, the size of dump trucks, are loaded down with toys and snacks of every imagin-able size and shape, those in tow seem to constantly squeal for some-thing else.

The people I really feel sorry for are those men and women who do business traveling every day. I have great admiration for them as they make a living making deals and catching planes. They are wired from head to foot with cell phones, laptops and the latest other gadgets that keep them tethered to their homes and businesses.

They couldn't pay me enough. I would lose my mind. The people they work so hard to support should appreciate what they go through each day they are on the road.

There were hoards of obese people with armloads of super-sized food items and hundreds of foreign visitors roaming around with a lost-in-space look on their faces. There were manic, uniformed youth groups who demanded to be noticed, drunken conventioneers and tired flight attendants giving their smiling muscles a rest. There were soldiers who proudly strutted in their creased uniforms. There was even a saffron-robed Buddhist monk checking out the girlie magazine in the gift shop.

There were people in sleazy outfits, people in high-fashion wardrobes and people who could have cared less about how they looked.

And best of all, I sat there knowing that God was also looking at all this and loving it.

April 14, 2005

Milking Life for All It's Worth

The glory of young men is their strength,
and the dignity of old men is gray hair.
Proverbs 20:29

Next week, on the 28th, I will celebrate my 61st birthday. I choke just seeing it in print. Even though 61 is not all that old, it is beginning to dawn on me that, yes, it is possible for even me to get old.

There are always a few people more than willing to remind me of my age. Often when I am sitting down to lunch, even with 40-year-old seminarians, they will casually mention their parents being 60 or 61. I spew soup all over them as they unconsciously remind me that I could have kids their age.

I have 35 years of priesthood down and only nine more years to go before retirement at 70. If possible, I plan to keep working as a priest even after 70, but the question that is on my mind on this birthday is this, "What do I want to do with the next nine years, presuming my health stays good?"

Most of all I want to live until I die. I do not want to become one of George Bernard Shaw's "feverish little clods of grievances and ailments." I want to follow the words of Dylan Thomas: "Do not go gently into that good night. Old age should burn and rave at close of day. Rage, rage against the dying of the light."

I want to keep believing the words, again George Bernard Shaw's: "This is the true joy in life, the being used for a purpose recognized by yourself as a mighty one; the being thoroughly worn out before you are thrown on the scrap heap." I want to milk life for all it's worth. I want to die with my boots on.

With that said, if God were to call me home in the near future, it would be OK. I have done more, been more places, met more people and accomplished more than I ever imagined I could. Priesthood has been the joy of my life. I am happy that God gave me the grace not to be like "George Gray," a poem I put in my spiritual journal many years ago. That poem is a map for me of how not to live.

"For love was offered me and I shrank from its disillusionment; sorrow knocked at my door, but I was afraid; ambition called me, but I dreaded the chance. Yet all the while I hungered for meaning in my life. And now I know that we must lift the sail and catch the winds of destiny wherever they drive the boat. To put meaning in one's life may end in madness, but life without meaning is the torture of restlessness and vague desire — it is a boat longing for the sea and yet afraid."

In short, I would like to come to the end my life with no regrets, no blame and filled with gratitude.

April 21, 2005

Our Stomachs are Full;
Our Hearts are Empty

You should be working for food that remains unto life eternal. John 6

I find lay Catholics ravenous for spiritual food. Their appetites are big, but there are not enough places they can go to be fed to satisfaction. Seeking alternatives to their unsatisfactory experiences in parishes, and disenchanted with the look of spirituality they find there, Catholics are now crossing religious lines, denominational lines and even state lines to find spiritual nourishment. Feed them and they will come. Don't feed them and they will leave.

I know this to be true from personal experience. From 1983-1997 I was pastor of our Cathedral. In those 14 years, we grew from 100 people to more than 2,100 by specializing in preaching and liturgy out of the book, done well. They crossed parish boundaries, diocesan boundaries and even denominational boundaries.

In our Gospel reading today, we are presented with a crowd of hungry people, people hungry more for stomach bread than spiritual bread. Their search for stomach bread is understandable. People then lived just one step ahead of starvation. Bread was everything. In their hunger, they went to great lengths to fill that hunger: they waited all day, walked for miles and rowed across a lake, in hopes of getting some more free bread.

People today, especially in our country, throw bread away. We have too much to eat. Obesity is a growing problem, even among the young. Our stomachs are full, but our hearts are empty. People are foraging for spiritual food, and when they cannot find good spiritual food, they will settle for whatever they find.

I get irritated when I hear our Catholics leaders condemn "new age spirituality." It is easier to condemn than it is to inspire. Can they not understand that the sterility of organized religion is what gave birth to the "new age movement"? In too many eyes, our churches are as dry as dust.

Catholics, I believe, are sick of our liberal-conservative obsession with church organization forms, while we neglect the essence of the Christian faith — personal discipleship. In my class for the soon-to-be-ordained, I stress that they be first of all spiritual leaders. They can give away the management functions of a parish, but they must not fail to develop their own spiritual leadership skills or fail to recognize the spiritual leadership ability of the laity.

"Nemo dat quod non habet." "If you don't have it, you can't give it." Our spiritual leaders must not only be good personally, they must be good at spiritual leadership. They must be spiritual persons themselves and spiritual teachers for others.

Our people are starving for solid spiritual food, not more organizational politics and liturgical changes. Our Catholic people are hungering and thirsting for holiness. We must prepare people to feed them and teach them to feed themselves. As Franklin D. Roosevelt said, "It is a terrible thing to look over your shoulder when you are trying to lead — and find no one there."

April 28, 2005

Should we Lower our Standards or Try Harder?

This sort of talk is hard to endure. How can anyone take it seriously? From this time on, many of his disciples broke away and would not remain in his company any longer.
John 6:60,66

From what I can make out in my reading of the Gospels, Jesus was a teacher who could hold people to the highest standards on one hand and shower them with tons of mercy and compassion when they failed to measure up to those high standards on the other. That, in my book, is very different from lowering standards and ideals simply because people failed.

The Scribes and Pharisees, on the other hand, held people to high standards as well, but they applied those high standards and ideals without mercy or compassion when people failed.

As a priest, I have spent a lot of time reaching out to Catholics who have been spiritually brutalized by those in the church who are too eager to judge and condemn, who apply the law without mercy.

On the other hand, I am aggravated by Catholics who are angry at "the church" because it will not lower its high standards when some people, even many people, cannot live up to them. Instead of changing their own behaviors to fit these ideals, they believe these high ideals ought to be changed to fit the reality of their failures.

Because we are more formed by Hollywood than the Gospels, this seems to come up most often in the area of divorce and remarriage. Should the church change its teaching on the permanence of marriage to fit our 55 percent divorce rate? Or should our 55 percent divorce rate be lowered to fit the high standards of the permanence of marriage taught by Jesus and upheld by the church? I believe we are the ones who need to do the changing.

I have made a pact with a good friend of mine that if I were ever to leave the priesthood (no plans whatsoever), that he would do whatever he could to stop me from writing one of those letters blaming "the church" for why I left.

I knew what I was getting into, and if I don't make it, I hope I will have the honesty to admit that I did not have what it took to stay with it instead of blaming "the church" for not changing its rules.

In these and other matters, I believe that we should do what Jesus did: hold to our high standards and pour on the compassion for those who fail. As a priest, it is my job to teach the truth of the Gospels as taught by the church and leave the judgment to God.

Personally, if I miss the mark, I would rather err on the side of mercy and compassion than on the side of severity and judgment. As the Letter of James (2:13) says, "Merciless is the judgment on the one who has not shown mercy; for mercy triumphs over judgment."

May 5, 2005

Thirty-Five Years as a Priest

Were not our hearts burning within us while he spoke to us on the way and opened the Scriptures to us? Luke 22:32

I can hardly believe it, but I will celebrate my 35th anniversary as a priest on May 16. All these years seem to have gone by so quickly. I think it is safe to say that I am well past the halfway mark.

One of the ordination presents that I still have seems to symbolize these first 35 years of priesthood. It is a piece of modernistic, green pottery from Spain, a stylized sculpture of a priest.

My ceramic priest wears a cassock with buttons from neck to feet. He wears a broad-brimmed, European-style hat. He clutches a book of the Gospels. It was given to me by an old friend, Jack Anderson, and I have dragged it with me from one assignment to the next.

I have always loved this piece of pottery, but like me, it has seen a bit of wear and tear in all those moves. I have dropped it or knocked it over several times and have had to glue a few pieces back on. His broad-brimmed hat has a huge chunk missing. One of his eyes has been knocked out. Other than that, he still stands tall, seemingly oblivious to the beating he has endured over the years.

On my 35th anniversary, this chipped piece of pottery reminds me of myself. I have been knocked around a few times over the years, but I am still standing. I think I will keep him, no matter how many more times he gets nicked and chipped.

How I got from May 16, 1970 to May 16, 2005 is truly amazing. There is no explanation other than a "vocation," the proverbial call from God. I knew when I was seven that I wanted to be a priest. I acted on that knowledge at age 13 when I came to the old St. Thomas Seminary out on Brownsboro Road in Louisville. After six years there, I went to Saint Meinrad Seminary, where I now teach, for six more years.

I was finally ordained at age 26 after being in the seminary exactly half my life. I have absolutely no regrets. I am more than happy. I am eternally thankful for the opportunities that came to me because of that decision.

I have been blessed with diverse and wonderful assignments. I have lived with the people of Somerset, Monticello, Whitley City, Calvary, Louisville and now the monks of Saint Meinrad Archabbey and Seminary. I have been a pastor, vocation director, college teacher, campus minister, mission preacher, retreat director, spiritual writer and seminary mentor.

I have lived with some great priests: Fathers Thomas Buren, Jerry Timmel, Lawrence Lindle, Bill Griner, Bill Medley, Joe Vest, Peyton Badgett, Marty Linebach and Archbishop Kelly.

As an old Gospel song puts it, "I wouldn't take nothin' for my journey now." Thanks be to God!

May 12, 2005

Some "Snapshots" of the Early Church

Their disagreement was so sharp that Paul and Barnabas separated. Acts 15:39

The family picture album is a very important part of remembering and sharing family histories: births, baptisms, first Communions, confirmations, birthdays, graduations, anniversaries, Thanksgivings, Christmases, Halloween parties, vacations and proms.

As wonderful as a family picture album is, it never tells the whole story. Unless your family was weird, you never grabbed the camera to get a shot of Mom when she was diagnosed with cancer, a shot of Dad in a drunken rage, uncles and aunts not speaking to each other, old girlfriends who didn't work out, or the looks on your parents' faces when your unmarried sister got pregnant.

The Acts of the Apostles is an album of snapshots of the early church. We read that beautiful passage about everybody meeting for prayer and the breaking of bread, sharing everything in common and attracting members every day. Acts, unlike most family albums, is disarmingly honest.

Not everything was sweetness and light, and if we keep reading, we will see that other side of the very early church.

We have bickering. We read that people sold their possessions and divided them according to each one's need, but we also read that the Greek-speaking widows complained that the Hebrew-speaking widows were getting a disproportionate share of that division.

We have cover-ups. Ananias and Sapphira sold their property and gave it to the church, holding back some of the proceeds, and then lied about it. They both dropped dead.

We have fanaticism. Saul was rounding up Christians and having them jailed for heresy, even holding the coats of those who stoned St. Stephen to death.

We have corruption. Simon, amazed that the Holy Spirit was being conferred by the laying on of hands, saw a gold mine of opportunity. He offered money for that power.

We have confrontation. Paul calls Peter "two-faced" for acting one way around Jewish converts and another around Gentile converts.

These are a few of the not-so-flattering snapshots of the early church that Scripture has the courage to include.

We read about Paul and Barnabas taking young John Mark with them on one of their missionary trips. If you stopped reading at that passage, you would miss the fact that John Mark got cold feet and came home.

On the next trip out, Barnabas wanted to forgive John Mark and try him again. Paul refused. They had a few strong words, and behold, the first team ministry ended in a fight. Unable to resolve their disagreement, Paul and Barnabas split up.

If we imagine the church was perfect in its infancy or during some period in our recent history, we can actually get a distorted picture of the church today. I believe those who criticize the church because it is "not like it used to be" simply do not know how the church "used to be." The fact is the church is "semper reformanda" — "always in need of reform."

May 19, 2005

Dealing with Critics of the Church

Be ready to give an explanation for the reason for your hope, but do it with gentleness and reverence. 1 Peter 3:15,16

It comes out of nowhere when you least expect it — an angry verbal attack by people who are upset with the church.

I still remember my first serious challenge. Newly ordained, I was attending a reception. Seeing my Roman collar from across the room, a young man made his way over and yelled in a loud, angry voice, "Why are you wasting your time in that stupid church? I finally wised up and got out of that silliness a long time ago. I can't believe that anyone as intelligent as you appear to be is still a Catholic, much less a priest."

I stood there, jaw dropped, as if I had been shot at close range. When he saw that I did not turn and run, he proceeded to go through his obviously well-rehearsed litany of all that is wrong with organized religion in general and the Roman Catholic Church in particular.

He covered the Inquisition, the Crusades, Galileo, the infallibility of the pope, the repression of women, child abuse, dull Masses, money-grubbing TV evangelists, all that "Vatican wealth" and the nun who slapped him in the second grade. I think I got blamed for everything but Tammy Faye's eye-liner.

This was only the first challenge. These challenges have increased over the last 35 years. In fact, I have seen the tables completely turned. When I was growing up, unbelievers were forced to defend themselves. Now believers are having to do the defending.

These challenges and questions have increased since the sexual abuse scandal. "Why stay in the church? Why not join a Protestant church? Why belong to a church that protected abusers and excludes women? Why stay when our church leaders seem so entrenched and inflexible? Why not join a religion that lets you believe what you want?" Maybe worse than these questions is the yawing look that discounts all that we hold dear.

My answer is simple. I agree with these critics. I agree that the church is riddled with sins and imperfections. I agree that the church has to own up to a long list of embarrassments. Where I disagree is what to do about it. I know the church's sins, but I also know its founder.

Jesus founded this church and promised to be with it till the end of time. He promised that it would be riddled with human weakness, but "even the gates of hell shall not prevail against it."

I am pained by my own sins and the sins of others in the church, but it is still Christ's body in the world. He is with it. It will stand whether I stay or leave, whether you stay or leave. I know of no church, especially one as old and big as this one, that does not have, or will not have, these same problems.

May 26, 2005

Doubt is not the Opposite of Faith

When the eleven disciples saw Jesus,
they worshipped, even as they doubted.
Matthew 28

"They worshipped Jesus even when they doubted." That's pretty much the opposite of what we do. When we doubt, we tend to quit worshipping. We assume that worshipping is only for believers.

The first thing many people assume about faith is that doubt is the opposite of faith. Not true. Honest doubt is not the opposite of faith. Honest doubt is actually an integral part of faith.

"They worshipped, even as they doubted." More important than whether doubt is part of faith is what to do about doubt. Many, when they doubt, remove themselves from worship. They say to themselves, "It is hypocritical for me to pretend to believe when I really don't believe. When I start believing, when my faith is strong, then it will make sense for me to start praying and worshipping."

That may sound good, even reasonable, but that's not how it works. As the disciples teach us, what really works is for us to "pray through" our doubt, to worship until we believe.

"They worshipped, even as they doubted." This may be yet another version of the great truth: "Fake it till you make it." Even though Alcoholics Anonymous made that idea famous, it actually goes back to the ancient Roman poet, Ovid, who said, "Pretend to be what is not, and then you'll become in truth what you are pretending to be." The great philosopher William James put it this way, "Act as if, and the mind will produce your desire."

The idea is, if you take something that feels impossible, or at least completely unnatural, and pretend that it is the easiest, most natural thing in the world for you to be doing, eventually it will become as easy as you're pretending it to be.

I practice this often in my own life. I grew up pretty much crippled by bashfulness. Bashful people find it painful to be in public situations. To cope, they try to avoid public situations as much as possible. This is a sure way to keep bashfulness going. The solution is to get out in public and fake confidence. You cannot think your way out of bashfulness; you have to act your way out.

When I was sent to southeastern Kentucky as a newly ordained priest, I decided to "fake it till I made it." Since I did not get what I wanted - which was not to be sent to southeastern Kentucky - I decided to pretend to want what I got until I was able to really want what I got. By acting as if it was a great assignment, it became a great assignment.

My friends, all of us have a good measure of doubt, even as we believe. The secret to a stronger faith is to act as if we have a strong faith until our faith is strengthened, to worship until we want to worship. Even believers sometimes have to "fake it 'til they make it."

June 2, 2005

Staying Connected with God

He is like a tree planted near running water
whose leaves never fade. Psalm 1:3

I am far from being an expert, technologically speaking, but I do have a computer, a cell phone, a digital camera and something else. Next to my computer, the most useful gadget I own is my portable Magellan Road Mate 700 Global Positioning System.

As part of my job at Saint Meinrad School of Theology, I am required to travel to many of the dioceses we serve. I fly to some, but I drive to many others. One of the things that worried me when I started this job was driving around all those strange cities, by myself, while trying to read a map.

Thanks to my portable GPS, all I have to do is plug it into my cigarette lighter, turn it on, wait a minute or two until it connects to a series of twelve satellites, punch in an address, and the GPS displays the route and verbally directs me right to the front door. Even if I make a wrong turn, it immediately tells me and directs me back to where I needed to go.

It occurred to me the other day that a GPS is amazingly analogous to our lives as disciples of Jesus. A good disciple regularly connects to Jesus through prayer to receive direction and clarity in staying on the right track in living his or her life. A GPS is a symbolic, if not simplistic, way to explain our connection to the helping and guiding presence of God in our lives.

The ancients had other ways of describing this connection. They compared it to being like a tree planted near running water and a house built on rock. Unlike a tree planted in a desert, a tree planted near running water stays green, no matter how severe the drought, because it is connected by its roots to a constant supply of fresh water. Unlike a house built on sand, a house built on rock never has to worry about storms because it is solidly anchored.

No matter what your calling in life, the best way to live is to stay connected to God, to build your house on solid rock and to plant yourself by running water so that you can survive all of life's storms and droughts — not only survive, but thrive.

Organized religion is taking its punches these days, but organized religion is just an earthenware jar that holds a great treasure. Don't be so put off by the earthenware jar that you miss the great treasure it holds.

Stay connected to your faith community. Come back to this source when you lose your way, when you get lost. Be like a tree planted near running water. Be like a house built on rock. If you do that, you won't have to worry about droughts and storms. You can stand tall, even on the worst days.

June 9, 2005

What We Need are Conversions, not Crusades

Always be ready to give an explanation for your hope, but do it with gentleness and reverence. 1 Peter 3: 15,16

Blessed Pope John XXIII, one step away from sainthood, said in his speech to open Vatican Council II, "The church has always opposed errors. Frequently, she has condemned them with the greatest severity. Nowadays, however, the spouse of Christ prefers to make use of the medicine of mercy rather than severity. She considers that she meets the needs of the present day by demonstrating the validity of her teaching rather than by condemnation."

He sounds very Jesus-like to me, but some very vocal people in our church are claiming that "the medicine of mercy" didn't work; that it almost destroyed the "real church." They are trying to tell us that we need to go back to severity and condemnations before the whole church falls apart.

Not everyone who speaks out forcefully in the name of "truth" is a prophet. Nasty, judgmental and hateful are not synonyms for prophetic. Unlike true prophets who speak the truth with love, these people merely like to hear themselves rant and rave, thinking they can demonstrate their commitment by forcing commitment onto others.

A firm conviction alone does not necessarily make something so. One has only to think of those in the church in bygone days who were convinced that the Earth was flat and that the sun revolved around the Earth. Their certainty, and rigid defense of that certainty, did not make it so. Even Saul, who was convinced that he was doing God a favor by killing Christians to protect the old-time religion, had to be knocked off his high horse.

People who rant and rave about how the church ought to be listened to have already lost the war. What we need are conversions, not crusades. Conversion is the process of a heart changing that leads to a free embrace of the way of Jesus. Crusades are about forcing change onto people. Everyone should know by now that crusades don't work in the long run.

Jesus chose the changing-people path over the changing-things path. He invited people to change rather than forcing them to change. He chose to "demonstrate the validity of his teaching rather than condemnation."

What parishes need desperately today are people who are bridge builders, peacemakers, reconcilers and mediators of unity. Priests and lay ministers especially need to be able to deal constructively with diversity, pluralism, complexity, ambiguity, division and polarization. Our church needs people who are ministers of healing communion, people whose words heal rather than wound, people who can express themselves with sensitivity for the dignity and worth of every person.

The American bishops ("As One Who Serves") tell us: "The style of leadership on the part of the priest is one of service. He is to be a servant to the People of God, holding them accountable for what they have been and can be. Holding them accountable must be done with love and patience, never with anger or meanness".

June 16, 2005

Some Good Things that Get Little Attention

There is cause for rejoicing here. 1 Peter 1:6

I have an old copy of a book about the life of Father Charles Nerinckx, one of our famous Kentucky frontier priests. There is one quote of his that especially stands out for me: "He who presides over the keeping of the rules should be the first observer of them."

Perhaps these words capture why Catholic people are so angry at the way our leaders handled the sexual abuse situation.

The fact that we failed in a major way is obvious to all. What may not be obvious to all is that during this same period there were many good things going on in the church that did not get much attention. This fact became clear to me as I clicked on "statistics" at the U.S. Conference of Catholic Bishops' Web site and read down the page. Here is some of the good news and interesting facts about our church documented there.

There are 63.4 million Catholics in the United States, and we make up 23 percent of the total population. Of the 63.4 million Catholics, 39 percent are Hispanic. By 2020, more than 50 percent of all Catholics in the United States will likely be Hispanic. There are 2.3 million African-American Catholics and approximately 500,000 Native American Catholics.

There are about 19,000 parishes in the United States. The average parish has about 3,254 members, compared to 303 members in a typical non-Catholic congregation. The average Catholic parish grows about 10 percent every 10 years.

There are about 44,487 priests in the United States. There are 74,698 nuns, 5,568 religious brothers and 14,000 permanent deacons.

Of these, there are about 250 African-American priests, 300 sisters and 380 deacons. The average age of priests is 61. Nearly 500 new priests were ordained in 2003. Their average age was 36; 14 percent of them were Hispanic.

Because religious sisters traditionally worked for modest stipends or maintenance that did not include pension benefits, the average Social Security benefit for religious sisters today is $3,749 annually compared to $10,740 for other Americans.

Catholic Charities provides emergency services to about 5,353,376 people annually. This includes food, basic needs, shelter, disaster services, transitional housing, immigration services, summer camps for children, elderly care, disabled services and refugee settlement.

Catholic Relief Services, an overseas relief and development agency, provides direct aid to 62 million people in 91 countries in a typical year.

Catholic lay organizations such as the Knights of Columbus donate about $128.5 million and 60.8 million volunteer hours each year. The St. Vincent de Paul Society serves 14 million people every year, expending $335 million in monetary value of services. The Catholic Extension Society disburses $14 million each year to missionary dioceses in this country for evangelization.

This is just the tip of a large iceberg of good things happening in our church today that do not get a lot of attention from the press. As we face our shortcomings, let's not forget to celebrate the great good we do.

June 23, 2005

Loving the Sinner while Hating the Sin

Why does your teacher eat with tax collectors and sinners? Matthew 9

Why would a holy man, a rabbi, a religious teacher such as Jesus, hang out with, eat with and socialize with public sinners, riff-raff, failures and marginal personalities?

Surely he knew that such behavior would be misinterpreted, that people would talk, that it would appear that he was condoning their sin and that his reputation would be tarnished. The Gospel tells us that Jesus ate and drank with these religious losers so often that it earned him the nicknames of "glutton" and "drunkard."

Either he was naive and reckless, or else his actions were meant to send a message. When Jesus ate with tax collectors and sinners, he was not just slumming for the fun of it or merely shocking people to get their attention. He was sending a message, and his message was very simple: all people are created in the image and likeness of God. All people have dignity and worth in God's eyes, no matter what they do or fail to do.

By these actions, Jesus was teaching people that more important than their love for God was God's love for them. God's love, Jesus said in word and deed, was gratuitous — given without condition, given regardless. Jesus knew that those who experience this unconditional love would be led to conversion, freely choosing to change their ways to please God.

Jesus knew that the hair-splitting, gnat-straining theological discussions of religious authorities, their endless bickering over liturgical detail, their heartless judgment and angry polemics would never bring people's hearts to God. In fact, their approach was driving people further and further away from God.

By eating with tax collectors and sinners, the scum of church and society, Jesus sent them the message that God was willing to eat with them as well, and by eating with them he affirmed their basic dignity and worth. Jesus was the first to love the sinner while hating the sin.

Can you imagine how powerful that message was to people who had never felt good enough for God, people who had never been able to measure up, people who had always felt marginalized and kicked to the curb by the religious establishment? For them, the message of Jesus was indeed "good news." It was like stumbling onto a buried treasure or finding a gorgeous, rare pearl.

Preaching this message still threatens those who have anointed themselves as true preservers of our religious tradition. Sadly, it seems that these critics have not learned what Jesus knew, that judgment and condemnation might make the one doing the judging and condemning feel righteous, but it does not motivate sinners to change. It fact, it probably hardens them in their choice against change.

The real reason Jesus ate with tax collectors and sinners was the fact that he knew, in the words of St. Francis de Sales, that "one drop of honey attracts more bees than a barrel of vinegar."

June 30, 2005

Deacons and their Wives
Often Unappreciated

*Select from among you seven reputable men,
filled with the Holy Spirit and wisdom, whom
we shall appoint to this task. Acts 6:3*

Recently, I led my third or fourth deacon retreat for the various deacon groups of our archdiocese. A couple of years ago, I had an opportunity to lead a day of prayer for the deacons of the Diocese of Lexington. Over the years, I have taught several courses in their training program.

My direct experience of working with deacons revolves mostly around Deacon Pat Wright, who served faithfully through the Cathedral of the Assumption, and Deacon Bob Hall, with whom I shared office space at the Maloney Center.

I cannot, of course, mention either of these great deacons without mentioning their spouses and partners in ministry, Sandy Wright and Cheri Hall. They represent many good deacons' wives and their heroic service work in our parishes and church organizations.

I single out of these two deacons and their partners as representative of many good deacons and their partners who are doing critical ministry throughout our diocese. They represent only the tip of a huge iceberg of good work that often goes unseen and unappreciated.

Several things amaze me about our local community of deacons and their wives. First of all, they sacrifice several years of weekends being trained for their ministries.

Second, they usually work as a husband and wife team, supporting, encouraging and helping each other in doing the difficult work of ministering to the sick, the elderly, the poor and the imprisoned.

Third, most of them carry out their ministry while trying to balance their marriages, their families and full-time jobs.

Fourth, most carry out their ministry without pay and, worse, sometimes without much appreciation.

There seem to be at least two misconceptions about the ministry of deacons. The first misconception is that deacons are assistants to priests, people to be brought in where priests are lacking. Deacons and priests have their own specific gradated participation in the office of the bishop. Deacons represent one arm of the bishop and priests the other. Deacons are not subordinate to priests but to the bishop directly. Each has different and specific ministries, and they collaborate with each other.

The second misconception is that deacons are meant to perform the service work of the church. In truth, deacons are not meant to perform all the service ministries of the church, nor could they. They are meant to inspire, motivate and train others for service work. It is the deacon's role to be on the front line, to be an attentive listener and to pay attention so as to lead the church's response to the service needs of the church and world.

The diaconate, like all ordained ministry, is to equip others for service. It is not meant to suppress and crush other ministries, but rather to call all of us to carry out our share of service to the world.

Thanks to all our deacons and their partners.

July 7, 2005

Sometimes It's Hard to Keep on Caring

At the sight of the crowds, Jesus' heart was moved with pity because they were troubled and abandoned. Matthew 9:36

Country music has a way of explaining things in common, everyday language that often would take professionals pages to explain. Take the concept of "compassion fatigue," for instance. There is a hit country song that explains that concept quite simply. The song is called "My Give a Damn is Busted."

"Compassion fatigue" refers to a physical, emotional and spiritual fatigue or exhaustion that takes over a person and causes a decline in his or her ability to feel and care for others. Emergency care workers, counselors, mental health professionals, medical professionals, advocate volunteers, human service workers, clergy and pastoral professionals are especially vulnerable.

Jesus is often presented in the Gospels as a person deeply moved by the suffering of others. When Jesus said "blessed are those who mourn, blessed are those who have the ability to feel deeply for others," he was first of all referring to himself.

The strongest word in the Greek language for what Jesus felt in the reading cited above is "splagchnisthesis," from the Greek word for "bowels." It is a degree of caring that comes from the depths of one's being. In the Gospels, Jesus is often moved with this kind of pity.

He was moved to the depths of his being when he looked out over the spiritually bewildered crowd, when he was confronted by crowds hungry for bread, when the master faced his servant who was in debt over his head, when Jesus noticed the two blind men sitting alongside the road, when Jesus noticed a poor, shunned and suffering leper, when Jesus saw the only son of a widowed woman being carried to his grave, when the Samaritan came upon the beat-up man beside the road, when the love-sick father caught sight of his prodigal son and when Jesus saw Mary weeping over her brother Lazarus.

Nothing kills the ability to feel pity and compassion like being disappointed over and over again. When we end up living in a world of so many lies, broken promises, unfounded claims and unkept vows, we, too, can grow cold and cynical.

I am convinced that Jo Dee Messina's song is popular because she sings about feelings so many people have these days. "You filled my head with so many lies, twisted my heart till something snapped inside. I really wanna care. I want to feel somethin'. Let me dig a little deeper — nope — sorry — nothin'."

Caring takes a lot out of the one doing the caring. Sometimes, the one caring "snaps" and becomes numb in the face of caring again. We live in a world in which we are bombarded constantly by the media with images of poverty and violence. They bring us to the point where we are tempted to shut down.

Christians, too, may get to the point where they feel their "give a damn is busted," but they must never give into those feelings for long.

July 14, 2005

The People of Small Parishes are Special

God saw how good it was. Genesis 1:18

A few weeks ago, I was privileged to accept an invitation from the people of the now-closed "Little St. Joe" parish in Marion County to celebrate a homecoming Mass in the old cemetery with Deacon Joe Dant at my side. Even though they are technically no longer a parish, the people there have turned the old church property into a community center and museum.

Like many of our rural parish communities who do not expect much attention from an urban-oriented Catholic church, they seemed genuinely shocked that I said "yes" to their invitation. Barry Brady, the chief organizer of the event, told me that when I returned his call he was on his bicycle. He said he was so surprised and shocked he had to pull over the side of the road.

Being from an old, small, Catholic community myself, I could not resist. I try to go out of my way to encourage these little pockets of old Catholicism whenever I can. The depth of their appreciation manifested itself when I entered their little museum. Just for being there, they had hung a large picture of me among their sacred treasures with the label "Home Coming 2005."

The first thing I encountered was the welcome I got from people all over Marion County. Though I was in Calvary, Ky., for only three and a half years and left 22 years ago, they always treat me as if I left last year.

The second thing I encountered was the great number of people who told me that they read this column every week, even people I did not know. They appreciate what they call my "simple, down-to-earth style." Several told me that there is a serious rumor going around down there that I was going to be the next bishop. I rushed to assure them that the clergy shortage had not reached such a critical level yet.

The third thing I encountered was a great devotion to their former pastor, Father Ernie Shumacher. Two men took me to his gravesite and spoke of him with great reverence, saying that he should be canonized. He symbolizes a great truth I often share with seminarians: if you love your people, they will love you, no matter your shortcomings.

The fourth thing I encountered was a very young father and his daughter. When he gave me his name, "Zoeller," I asked if he was related to the woman in the fresh grave I had just seen. It was his young wife who had just recently died of cancer. He told me that he had grown to appreciate what single mothers have to go through. My heart went out to him.

I came home amazed at the enduring faith of these people and the faith of people in the many small country parishes around our diocese. If you were born and raised in one of these small parishes, as I was, you know just how special these people are.

July 21, 2005

Pray to Keep the Priests we Have

Fan into flame the gift God gave you when
I laid hands on you. 1 Timothy 1:6

I don't know which is harder, getting to ordination or staying in the priesthood. I struggled through 12 years of seminary. I have struggled just as hard over the last 35 years to stay a happy and effective priest. By the grace of God, I am still a priest and quite happy at it.

Just as is the case with marriage, ordination is not magic. Both vocations require constant vigilance and nurturing. Ministry is hard work, and giving up on it has been a temptation from the very beginnings of the church.

In the reading cited above, Paul is writing to young Timothy, who is so discouraged that he wants to quit and come home. He bids Timothy to "fan into flame the gift God gave you when hands were laid on you." It is in this passage that Paul wishes Timothy sophronismos, a favorite Greek word of mine meaning "the ability to keep one's cool in the face of panic."

As a vocation director, I worked as hard as I could to recruit good candidates for the priesthood. Now, as the founding director of Saint Meinrad's new Institute for Priests and Presbyterates, I am working hard to help keep the priests we have and to offer our new, young pastors some practical help.

This is very important work. According to a recent study by Dean Hoge, we have a growing shortage of new priests, and we are also losing 10 to 15 percent of our new priests within their first five years. We know why those who leave, leave, but Mr. Hoge is now doing a study of those ordained five to nine years ago to see why those who stay, stay.

Priests who leave within five years or less leave because of loneliness and feelings of being overwhelmed and unappreciated. Twenty-eight percent of all American priests now live alone, some for the first time in their lives. Young priests are now being made pastors of one, two and sometimes three parishes within a year or two of ordination, often without much preparation or support.

The makeup of presbyterates, the entire body of priests in a particular diocese, is also changing. We are no longer the cohesive group of locally born, same-age and consistently trained individuals we once were. Twenty-seven percent of all American priests are foreign-born. Seventeen percent are converts to Catholicism. There are many older second-career men, widowers and even married former ministers.

Our Institute for Priests and Presbyterates is trying to offer practical help for priests in ministry across diocesan lines, as suggested by Pope John Paul II. We hope to offer ongoing formation for individual priests, especially those who are moving out of the seminary and into their first years of ministry, as well as ongoing formation of whole presbyterates.

Pray for more priests, but we also pray for our effort to keep those we do have.

July 28, 2005

Faith is a Garden that Needs Regular Attention

The seed sown in rich soil is the one who hears the word and understands it, who indeed bears fruit. Matthew 13:23

A few weeks ago, one of my Record column readers was disappointed that I had stated that doubt was not the opposite of faith but an integral part of a healthy faith. I stand by what I said and respect his right to see it from another angle.

Because I believe that what I said is true, I tend to attract people who are struggling with their faith, not the super-convinced. The super-convinced people who don't seem to have any doubts usually don't like what I have to say.

I heard from one of my struggling believer friends recently who confessed to having "drifted" after coming back to church for a few years. He'd been away from the church for many years before that.

He really is more spiritually healthy than he knows. He did not blame "the church" for any of it. He admitted that he had not been invested in his spiritual life and had grown lax in church attendance and spiritual practice.

In the words of the parable cited above, he was not doing the work of tilling the soil of his life to receive God's word. Like the seed that landed among the thorns, his recent joyful return to church had lasted only a few years. The busy-ness of life and other worldly concerns had "choked the Word and was no longer bearing fruit."

This parable has a lot to teach us.

Sometimes God comes into our lives, and we give him no reception. We are like the packed-down earth of a footpath. The seed of God's Word has no chance of taking root. It bounces off us. We just don't "get it" when it comes to religion or spirituality.

Sometimes when God comes into our lives, we give him a great reception as long as things are going well. But then scandals, persecutions and infighting in the church provide us an excuse to drop out. We are "fair-weather" disciples. Our "faith" withers in the heat of the day.

Sometimes God comes into our lives, and we give him a great reception. We have good intentions of walking the spiritual path, but we get overly involved in other things. Soon our faith shrivels.

And sometimes God comes into our lives, we give him a great reception, and each year we grow deeper and deeper in our understanding of and relationship to God and his holy Word. We live our faith and watch it produce great things in our lives.

Faith is a gift, yes, but it requires constant vigilance and cultivation, much like tending a garden. Like a garden, if we want fresh vegetables and beautiful flowers, we have to work with God. If we don't, we should not expect a rich spiritual life. God is doing his part; now we need to do ours.

August 4, 2005

A New Place with a New View
of the World

Do you have eyes and not see? Mark 8:18

I recently sold my house and moved into a condo. Because my job at Saint Meinrad Archabbey requires that I live there at least four days a week and because of my work at Bellarmine University — and helping out in parishes, too — I no longer have time to deal with cutting grass, raking leaves and keeping plants watered.

One good thing about a move is that it offers another view of the world, a new set of people to watch and write about. From my deck I can see the sidewalk that leads from Parkway Medical Center to the corner of Poplar Level and Eastern Parkway. I regularly see nurses, aides and various support staff from that nursing home and Norton Audubon Hospital dragging their tired bones up the sidewalk to catch the bus home.

Talk about people who need an encouraging word. While a few at the top of the health-care food chain are making obscene amounts of money, most of these people are trying to support families on very low wages while often doing demeaning work that most people could not or would not do.

They give wrinkled old strangers baths, empty their bedpans and clean them up after mishaps. They listen to endless jabber, tedious requests and constant complaints. If we paid them what they are worth, I suppose health care would go further through the roof.

Tired to the bone, you can see them dragging their feet as they walk in the rain and in heat to wait for a bus to take them home and to another day's work at home. My heart goes out to them.

I notice them mainly because I was one of them during the summer when I was a college seminarian. I used to walk home to my rented basement apartment, down Eastern Parkway, from my jobs at St. Joseph Infirmary. I worked seven days a week: on the grounds crew, in the chapel, in the emergency room and sometimes at the front desk.

On a minimum wage, I could barely pay my rent, eat and save up enough spending money to last me through the seminary school year. I lived in the world of wanting, but not having. I ate at White Castle three times a day and pigged out on payday at the "all you can eat for $5" seafood deal at the old Howard Johnson. I could barely take care of myself. There is no way I could have supported a family, even with three jobs.

I have always thought that the best way to be a priest is to first of all be a real person, one who lives with the people he serves. When he is "out of touch" with ordinary people, he neither sees them nor feels for them. When that happens, he ceases to be that bridge between God and people that a priest is called to be, no matter how "holy" he may feel.

August 11, 2005

Cell Phone Use Could Be
a Sign of Loneliness

He withdrew in a boat to a deserted place
to be by himself. Matthew 14:13

I fought it as long as I could — but I've bought a cell phone and turned it on. At work, I find that I am wasting too much time miscommunicating. Cell phone users aggravate me, and here I am hating myself for caving in and joining them.

This move has caused me to dig deeply to try to understand why I am growing more irritated at the very sight of people blabbing endlessly on cell phones almost everywhere I look.

What aggravates me is not just the incredibly bad manners, but from what I can hear many of these people do not seem to have a single thought without having the need to communicate it to somebody, whether they are in the car, in the grocery, in restaurants or even in church.

It seems to me that the explosion of cell phones, along with portable headsets, pornography, dating services and recreational drugs, are mere symptoms of just how lonely we are in our culture. We are conflicted with competitive individualism and isolation on one hand and constant advertising that promotes the ideals of togetherness, unity and community on the other. Uncomfortable with being alone, even for a few minutes, we are driven to connect in whatever way we can.

I recently witnessed a meeting of young adults taking a break. As they poured out the door, nearly all of them flipped open their cell phones to call somebody. Having had to sit and listen without talking for a whole hour, they obviously needed relief.

Henri Nouwen makes this insightful point: "Our culture has become most sophisticated in the avoidance of pain, not only our physical pain but our mental and emotional pain as well. We have become so used to this state of anesthesia that we panic when there is nothing or nobody to distract us.

"By running away from our loneliness and by trying to distract ourselves with people and special experiences, we are in danger of becoming unhappy people suffering from many unsatisfied cravings and tortured by desires and expectations that never can be fulfilled."

What is the solution? Simply put, it is facing our loneliness rather than running from it. We cannot conquer loneliness until we get an inner life, and we cannot have an inner life without facing down silence and learning to enjoy our own company. Once we do this, we can actually learn to be alone without being lonely.

The loneliness monster afflicted me especially in my early years as a priest. I had no choice about living alone, but I learned that I did have a choice about whether it was going to make me lonely. Now, many years of practice later, I go bonkers without long stretches of being by myself and being quiet.

Maybe this is why these noise-makers irritate so much. They are stealing something sacred from all of us.

August 18, 2005

Coming to Terms with our Personal Histories

Can anything good come out of Nazareth? John 1:46

Last night, as I sat on my deck thinking about growing up in Rhodelia, Ky., a realization hit me like a ton of bricks: My God, I'm a Walton. Like the Walton kids on TV, my four sisters, two brothers and I grew up in a small town with a country store-gas station-post office, all rolled into one.

My grandfather and grandmother on my dad's side didn't actually live with us, but they did live directly across the road. We had the run of both houses. My grandmother even crossed the road to deliver me and performed an emergency baptism when I was born.

We raised a garden and canned vegetables. We raised chickens and slaughtered them ourselves. We raised hogs and had them butchered. We went fishing and played barefoot in the woods. I even took my turn milking the cow.

Just as the Waltons did, my granddad and father owned a sawmill and filled orders for rough lumber to build barns and farm buildings. My dad eventually turned the sawmill into a successful building material business as I got older, but during the 40s and 50s, Rhodelia was very much like Walton's Mountain.

Like John-Boy himself, I was the oldest son and the first in my family to go off to college and graduate. Yes, sir, down deep I am a Walton.

Sooner or later, we all have to come to terms with our personal history. We have to choose to embrace it or reject it. Today, after working through some early seminary experiences, I am happy to say that I have embraced my roots.

As a high school seminarian, those of us from the country had to endure the teasing of our city classmates. They even used Scripture against us. "Can anything good come out of Nazareth?" Outnumbered, some of us were hesitant to share much about our rural roots, lest we give them more fuel for teasing.

Today, I am happy to say I am proud of my roots. One of the things I am most proud of is my family, my two brothers and four sisters. Of course, we gossip about each other a little, but we get along wonderfully. We stay in contact and get together whenever we can, especially before Christmas when we gather to share a meal and celebrate a home Mass.

We pray for our dead parents, laugh non-stop, talk all at once and have a great time together, going over the same old stories. My poor brothers-in-law have to sit back and witness this annual spectacle.

Each year I remind them of how many siblings cannot get together because of the divisions among them. I also remind them that maybe next year one of us could be missing, so we should enjoy each other while we are all still here.

What about your family? If there's something you need to do before it's too late, do it today.

August 25, 2005

"All Are Welcome! All Are Welcome!"

My house shall be called a house of prayer
for all people. Isaiah 56:7

I have a needlepoint pillow on my recliner with a quote from Mark Twain that says, "If I cannot smoke cigars in heaven, then I shall not go." If I knew how to sew, and had the patience and time, I would like to create a bigger pillow that would read, "If the only people allowed in heaven are religious fanatics, then I shall not go."

One of the things that sends me up the wall quicker than anything these days are the fundamentalist types who cannot resist the temptation to pronounce authoritatively just whom God loves and whom he doesn't love.

They probably started out speaking humbly about God but have ended up speaking arrogantly for God. It is one the biggest traps a seriously religious person can fall into. Their philosophy is summed up in a humorous bumper sticker I once saw, "I'm saved! Sorry about you!"

I am proud of at least one of my bright ideas — inviting people to dedicate a gold-leaf star on the blue ceiling of the Cathedral. I am proud, as well, of the marble pulpit that the parishioners of the Cathedral dedicated to me toward the end of my tenure. It is actually the bishop's pulpit, of course, but as his representative I was privileged to preach an inclusive message of God's universal and unconditional love from it for 14 years.

That inclusive pulpit stands under an inclusive heaven. People have dedicated stars on behalf of Catholics, Protestants and Jews; the religiously observant and those who have dropped out; the rich and the poor; people of various races and ethnic groups; people who are gay and people who are straight.

Even the Dalai Lama, a Buddhist, and a rabbi or two have stars in that heaven. I like to think I left my mark there, on pulpit and ceiling, a mark that says, in the words of a hymn we sing quite often, "All are welcome! All are welcome — in this place."

Because of this, there has been a steady stream of critics who think that a good priest and a good Catholic would be culling sinners and condemning heretics, not handing gold stars to them.

Our church had a great breakthrough at Vatican Council II. While believing we teach the fullness of truth, we admitted that there is some truth in all religions, that all religious people who sincerely seek God deserve respect and, yes, that we can even learn something from them.

There are, unfortunately, zealots in our church today who would like to take all that back and replace it with the message that we are the only people with the truth and that others have nothing to offer but falsehood, ignorance and heresy. This thinking must be resisted wherever it rears its ugly head. If Pope John Paul II could pray in synagogues and mosques and Pope Benedict XVI can continue the practice, then people such as myself must be in good company.

September 1, 2005

Sometimes We Already
Know the Answer

There was a strong heavy wind, then an earthquake, then a fire, but the Lord was not in them. Then the Lord spoke in a tiny whispering sound. 1 Kings 19:11-13

In the counseling I have done and in the counseling I been through myself, it often seems that we already know, down deep somewhere, what we need to do. But all the external noise drowns out that wise but "tiny, whispering" voice in our own hearts.

All the counselor seems to do is to encourage us listen to that wise but tiny, whispering voice, God's voice, that leads us where we need to go.

Let me give you an example from my own life. After 14 years of being pastor of our Cathedral, I found that my body was experiencing unexplained rashes. My sleep was being interrupted; I continually felt exhausted and could not rally as I had always done in the past. I thought I was going crazy. I decided to go see a counselor.

After many hundreds of dollars and hours of talking, something came out of my mouth that surprised even me. I said to the counselor, not being very serious, "Well, maybe it's time for me to leave the Cathedral." When I said that, the counselor was quick to point out that I had sighed deeply and slumped back into the chair. I had my answer, and it was there all along. I just couldn't hear it.

I have found this to be true in my counseling of others as well. Those who report a "breakthrough" are those who knew the answer all along. I call that moment when we can hear that tiny, whispering voice in our own hearts the "ah ha" experience.

God is guiding each one of us with a tiny, whispering voice. The problem is not whether God is speaking to us but whether we can hear him above all the other screaming voices within us and around us.

Today, a whole generation of young people are living with noisy, outside, brainwashing voices pumped into their ears from the time they get up until the time they go to bed. The noise arrives through cell phones, headsets and huge car speakers that rattle windows for blocks around. Some even sleep with music lyrics and TV chatter in the background.

Why am I so surprised by the number of 30-year-olds I meet who still have no idea what to do with their lives? Maybe it's because they have never given themselves the opportunity to hear that wise voice in their own hearts that says, in the words of Isaiah, "This is the way; walk in it."

At our baptisms and confirmations, we were made temples of the Holy Spirit. Among the gifts of the Spirit are wisdom, understanding, knowledge and counsel. Deep within us this treasure chest of "answers" and "solutions" awaits our discovery. The access code is silence. We are much smarter than we realize.

September 8, 2005

Growing the Seeds God Planted In Us

Some seeds fell on the walkway, some on
rocky ground, some among the thorns, but
some fell on rich soil and produced fruit, a
hundred or sixty or thirty fold. Matthew 13

I grew up with the belief that life is something that happens to you,
and all you can do is to make the most of it.

Feeling victimized by a whole range of powerful forces, I ended up
as a teen-ager like a lot of people I know who have become, in the words
of George Bernard Shaw, "feverish little clods of ailments and grievances complaining that the world will not devote itself to making them
happy."

As I have written and spoken about many times, one day at the beginning of my junior year of college, I was standing on a fire escape
between classes with a classmate friend. Out of nowhere, it seemed,
these words came out of my mouth, "Pat, I am so sick and tired of being
bashful, backward and scared of life, I am going to do something about
it, even if it kills me."

It must have been a moment of grace, a gift from God, because from
that day on I decided to quit whining from the back seat of life and to
get behind the wheel. I decided to do hard things for my own good and
seize every opportunity I could to enrich my life.

It was not a magic decision, and the change did not come easily, but
that critical decision changed my life in ways that I could not have imagined. It may have been the most important decision I ever made, something I hope to practice until I am dead.

Jesus originally created the parable cited above as a way to talk about the different receptions people gave to the seeds of his teaching. I love this parable, because it has a very important message for all of us. God has wonderful seeds he wants to plant in us. We are the soil in which these seeds of opportunity are being sprinkled.

It occurred to me the other day that there is a growing number of people who are making a killing off pathetic people who have made bad choices. Suze Orman, the TV personal finance advisor, is raking it in explaining to stupid people that if you make $2 and spend $4, you are going to end up in trouble. Maury Povich is also raking it in by giving pathetic human examples of bad choices a stage to wallow in the consequences of their bad choices.

The thing that all these people have in common is their tendency to believe that they are helpless victims of bad luck and unfortunate circumstances rather than victims of their own bad choices.

Personal and spiritual suicide is the result of saying "no" to your opportunities to grow and change. You are up to your neck in God-given opportunities. Say yes.

September 15, 2005

Keeping Faith in the Church

You are Peter, and upon this rock I will build my church, and the gates of hell shall not prevail against it. Matthew 16

The question every Catholic has been forced to ask himself or herself these last couple of years is this: "Why stay a Roman Catholic with all the problems the church is having these days?"

I even received a letter recently from an old acquaintance of mine, a street person from my Cathedral days who is now "retired" in California. He said that he has a deep gratitude for the grace of perseverance but is saddened when he meets Catholics who "bailed out."

For me, there is a growing list of excuses to leave but one pressing reason to stay: this Gospel reading. Every Sunday of my life, I have recited our creed, in which I professed faith in "one, holy, catholic and apostolic church." By that, I mean that I have stated publicly, Sunday in and Sunday out, that I believe that the church of which I am a member is traceable, in a direct line, to Peter, head of the apostles, who died in Rome.

I believe that Pope Benedict XVI is the latest successor of Peter, on whom Christ built his church. But that does not mean that I am not aware that the church has always been afflicted from within and without with some awful personalities and behaviors.

I am saddened by the sins of the church, as well as my own sins. But I also know that the validity of the message we carry does not depend on the personal goodness of its messengers. There have been hated Popes as well as loved ones, but Christ's church is still handed from one generation to the next through the office of Peter. Therefore, I will trust this church.

There are lots of dreams and hopes being bantered about for the latest successor of Peter, Benedict XVI. I must admit that I, too, have my hopes for his ministry, even though mine are a little different from those of most people who have lists of things they hope he changes.

I am not as interested in him changing things nearly as much as I am in his ability to encourage and inspire faith in the hearts of ordinary Catholics, whether they have stayed or strayed.

We have been bickering about church organizational changes for so long that it seems the treasure is often neglected in favor of the crock. My hope is that this Pope will be able to inspire people to want to live the Christian life, not just choose sides in an ever-widening liberal-conservative war over religious forms.

In his new book about Pope Benedict XVI, John L. Allen may have said it best: "The Pope realizes that people are not convinced of the Christian message on the basis of doctrinal debates. They want to see that Christianity is a joyful thing, a source of life and hope that lights fires of love and self-sacrifice."

September 22, 2005